12 Steps To Better Exposition

Barbara Williams

Division of Continuing Education
University of Utah

CHARLES E. MERRILL PUBLISHING COMPANY
COLUMBUS, OHIO

A Bell and Howell Company

To J.D.
Who encouraged and indulged

ISBN 0-675-09660-X

Library of Congress Catalog Number: 68-15903

4 5 6 7 8 9 10 11 12 13 14 15-76 75 74

Printed in the United States of America

To the Teacher

I hope I have made this book flexible.

I have tried to include all the important elements of expository organization in the first nine steps for the benefit of students who must complete this basic study of rhetoric in a brief college quarter. But by including optional theme assignments for most of those nine steps and by providing additional explanation and examples on style (Steps 10-12), I intended to provide topics and assignments which would expand to a full semester's work.

The consideration of paragraph development as four separate steps will perhaps seem arbitrary. My purpose was to emphasize as constructively as possible a fundamental weakness in most student composition—anemic, underdeveloped paragraphs—without belaboring the problem indefinitely. If I have failed to state clearly enough that every piece of exposition need not employ all six methods of development considered in these four steps, perhaps you can supply my omissions—as indeed you may feel it necessary to do elsewhere.

For the ideas and examples in this book I am indebted to many people. First of all, I am grateful to my students who continually help me discard, temper, and improve my theories and methods. Secondly, I am appreciative of my fellow teachers who have given encouragement, offered suggestions, and supplied material from their own files: Mrs. Janet Booth, Mrs. Marie LeHolm, Mrs. Elaine McKay, Mrs. Carol Madsen, and Mrs. Emma Lou Thayne. But the biggest share of gratitude surely goes to Mrs. Kathleen Darley, Supervisor of Remedial English, Division of Continuing Education, University of Utah. Without her confidence, prodding, and careful reading of manuscripts, I should never have undertaken the project—much less seen it through to the end. Cheerful and competent clerical assistance was provided by Mrs. Joyce Howe. To her, too, I am sincerely indebted.

To the Student

If words flow from you like filament from a spider . . .

if committing your ideas to paper is effortless and delightful . . .

if you have already written The Great American Novel, or are working on it, or have it securely in mind . . .

in short, if you think composition is easy, and you always write successfully . . .

this book isn't for you.

This book is intended for those of you who chew more pencils than you write with, crumple more pages than you finish, and worry yourself to paralysis every time you are given a writing assignment. For you students perhaps this book can offer some help. It makes no guarantee of Pultizer prizes—just a little peace of mind and the self-confidence to produce written work that communicates the ideas you want it to and makes reading a pleasure.

Because most of the writing you will do in college will be explanation—how Elizabeth I succeeded or failed as a diplomat, why Paine's Crisis papers are still meaningful today, in what ways Willa Cather uses color and symbol—the emphasis here will be on how you go about explaining your ideas. Maybe you will discover in the process that writing is enjoyable and will want to go on for specialized courses in newswriting, short story writing, poetry writing, or playwriting.

But for now you will look only at writing that explains—that is, exposition.

Table of Contents

To the Teacher iii
To the Student v

Part I. Overcoming That Problem of Getting Started . 1

   Step 1. Planning the Thesis Statement 3
   Step 2. Enlarging the Pattern 13
         The Informal Outline 13
         The Formal Outline 19
   Step 3. Perfecting the Pattern 25
         How Should the Paper Begin? 25
         How Should the Paper End? 30
         How Will the Ideas Hang Together? 31
   Checklist for Patterns 39

Part II. Giving Your Paragraphs Substance 41

   Step 4. Letting the Topic Sentence Help You 43
   Step 5. Ordering Your Paragraphs 59
   Step 6. Using Detail and Illustration 70
   Step 7. Using Comparison/Contrast 77
   Step 8. Using Analysis and Definition 82
   Step 9. Using Reasons 92
   Checklist for Paragraphs 97

Part III. Separating the Flair from the Flapdoodle . . 99

   Step 10. How to Sidestep Wordiness and Vagueness . . 101
   Step 11. How to Use Figurative Language 122
   Step 12. How to Make Quotable Quotes 144
   Postscript on Style and Tone 170
   Checklist for Effectiveness 175

Index 177

PART I

Overcoming That Problem of Getting Started

Step 1. Planning the Thesis Statement

The first rule of good exposition can be put into a single word: **Plan.** Exposition, like a moon rocket or a house or even a hand-knit sweater, must begin with a pattern. And as a writer you will find that the simplest kind of a pattern is a *thesis statement*—a single sentence setting forth your purpose and point of view—which you carefully plan **before you begin to write.**

Any expository writing—that is, English themes, term reports, and informational papers of all kinds—must have some kind of underlying point or idea which you are trying to explain. That underlying idea, the *thesis,* may or may not be stated explicitly within the paper itself. If you do choose to spell out the thesis for your reader, you will probably put it in the first paragraph or the last—although when you gain experience, you are free to place it anywhere you care to. Occasionally (but only after you gain experience) you will not state the thesis in a particular sentence but merely suggest it in the paper as a whole.

Such fuzzy rules regarding the placement of a thesis may result in serious difficulties both in reading and writing. Students may read carelessly, allowing themselves to be sidetracked by incidental examples and details, without truly seeking the author's message. Or worse still, they may attempt to write exposition of their own which either has no thesis or does not stick to a *single underlying idea.*

3

Consider the following student theme:

Aunt Ellie

My great aunt Ellie, who is a spry little widow of nearly 80 years, is one of the most quick-witted people I have ever met. With the aid of her numerous jokes, her sparkling dialog, and her ability to laugh at any situation, she can always coax a person out of a glum mood, and I would rather spend an afternoon talking to Aunt Ellie than anyone else I can think of.

One of the most pleasant aspects of a visit to Aunt Ellie's house is the original refreshments she always serves. She never lets a guest leave her house without offering him something to eat, even if she can provide nothing more than stale bread and peanut butter. Of course her specialty is homemade peppermint ice cream, which she still manages to crank in an antique freezer.

I am 60 years younger than Aunt Ellie, but those old-fashioned hand freezers wear me out. I bought Mother an electric freezer for Christmas, but the ice cream it produces isn't very creamy. Nevertheless, ice cream is my favorite dessert, and I am glad we now own a freezer.

Aunt Ellie loves flowers and spends every waking moment from April through September working among her tulips, roses, petunias, and other blossoms. My sister in California has inherited Aunt Ellie's green thumb, and she has won several blue ribbons for her giant poinsettas. The climate is too cold for poinsettas in this part of the country.

Aunt Ellie lives in a well-kept bungalow which she classifies as "an authentic reproduction of synthetic early American." As a matter of fact, most people who buy early American houses and furniture really don't have any idea about how our forefathers actually lived.

I am sure you will agree that Aunt Ellie is an interesting person that anyone would want to spend an afternoon with.

This theme does contain a thesis, the second sentence in the first paragraph: *With the aid of her numerous jokes, her sparkling dialog, and her ability to laugh at any situation, she can always coax a person out of a glum mood, and I would rather spend an afternoon talking to Aunt Ellie than anyone else I can think of.* But the appearance of the thesis seems to be a matter of accident rather than design, for the student has disregarded its function as a pattern. Having stated that Aunt Ellie is pleasant to be with because of her jokes, dialog, and ability to laugh, the writer should illustrate these qualities—and these qualities only. *Any other material distracts from the thesis and should be eliminated.*

In diagram form the theme should look like this:

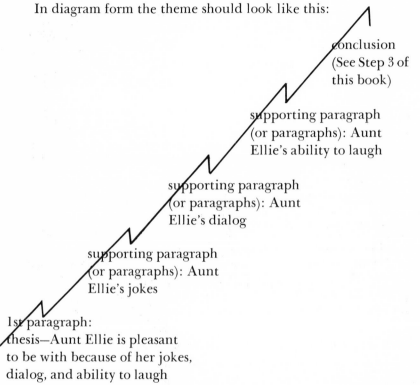

conclusion
(See Step 3 of
this book)

supporting paragraph
(or paragraphs): Aunt
Ellie's ability to laugh

supporting paragraph
(or paragraphs): Aunt
Ellie's dialog

supporting paragraph
(or paragraphs): Aunt
Ellie's jokes

1st paragraph:
thesis—Aunt Ellie is pleasant
to be with because of her jokes,
dialog, and ability to laugh

But what pattern does the Aunt Ellie theme actually follow? This paper is nothing but a string of aimless sentences, some less related to the thesis than others. Obviously the sentences about the writer's enjoyment of ice cream and his sister's green thumb do not belong in the paper. But neither does most of the material about Aunt Ellie. Only one sentence after the opening paragraph provides any evidence for the thesis. The first sentence in the fifth paragraph illustrates Aunt Ellie's wit and dialog and is therefore useful: *Aunt Ellie lives in a well-kept bungalow which she classifies as "an authentic reproduction of synthetic early American."*

But aside from the introduction itself, this is the only sentence which belongs in the theme.

An actual diagram of the Aunt Ellie theme might look like this:

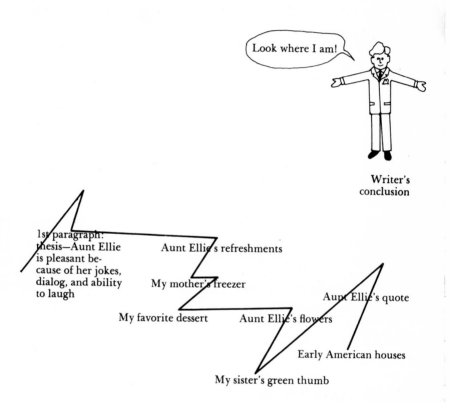

It is not quite clear how the writer of this theme reached the conclusion without taking the reader along. At best, an unmerited conclusion like this is trite and dull. At worst, it leads to argument and irritation.

PLANNING THE THESIS STATEMENT

The writer of the Aunt Ellie paper got himself into trouble because he did not consciously plan a thesis statement but instead set down an accidental thesis without realizing it. And despite how obvious the faulty structure of this sample paper may now appear to you, your own English teacher probably reads many themes each week which do not tightly focus on one clear underlying idea. However, you should have no real trouble avoiding this disastrous structural problem if you (1) can identify the difference between your topic and your thesis and (2) can recognize the qualities which make a good thesis statement.

The chart below points up the distinction between a topic (general subject) and a thesis (idea about a topic):

Topic	Improved Topic	Thesis Statement
College training in America	A comparison of Reed College and the University of California	Students at Reed College receive more personal attention than do students at the University of California.
The mail of a U. S. Senator	The crackpot mail received by a U.S. Senator	Much of a U. S. Senator's valuable time is spent answering crackpot mail.
My home town	The corner drugstore in my home town	The corner drugstore was the center of social life in my home town.

A thesis statement, therefore, narrows the topic and contains an idea or opinion about it. But other qualities are necessary as well for a good thesis statement:

A. Is marijuana really dangerous?
(Poor thesis statement. No opinion, merely a question.)
B. Marijuana may cause psychic if not physical dependence.
(Improved thesis statement. Complete sentence.)

A. Sky diving is great.
(Poor thesis statement. Too vague.)
B. Training in sky diving often justifies itself in rescue operations.
(Improved thesis statement. More specific.)

A. Education is necessary.
   (Poor thesis statement. Too obvious.)
B. College-trained people adjust better to stress situations than other adults.
   (Improved thesis statement. Not generally believed, but defensible.)
A. Swimming is the best sport in the world.
   (Poor thesis statement. Too emotional.)
B. Regular swimming keeps the entire body in good physical condition.
   (Improved thesis statement. Can be defended by reason.)

From these examples and the ones preceding you will see that

1. A good thesis statement is best expressed in a complete sentence (never a question).
2. A good thesis statement is clear.
3. A good thesis statement focuses on a narrow aspect of the topic.
4. A good thesis statement sets forth the writer's point of view.
5. A good thesis statement is not an obvious opinion which every reader already shares.
6. A good thesis statement can be defended by reason rather than emotion.
7. A good thesis statement sets the pattern for the paper to follow.

Whether they are beginning students or long-standing professionals, all careful writers of exposition will have their theses clearly in mind before they begin to write. But as a beginner you should do more than merely *think* about what you are going to say, or like the writer of the Aunt Ellie theme you may be diverted from your purpose during the course of composition. Until you gain experience, you will find the following rules helpful:

1. Write out the underlying idea of the paper in a complete sentence or *thesis statement.*

   This thesis statement is not a part of the composition. It is the pattern for the paper which you must bear constantly in mind in order to prevent the introduction of unrelated or contradictory material. Unless the teacher specifically asks to review the thesis statement, it will never be seen by anyone but you.

2. State the thesis in *another sentence within the composition,* as near the beginning of the paper as possible.

   This kind of a sentence at the beginning of a paper is called an *explicit deductive thesis* although it is not necessary for you to remember the term. Not until you have mastered the simple method of placing a thesis at the beginning should you attempt a paper in which the thesis is placed elsewhere or a paper which does not state the thesis at all.

Following these two rules will make the task of writing easier and will result in better prose. The thesis statement is not one more problem for you to worry about but a useful pattern that will lighten your burdens considerably.

Exercise

The Thesis Statement

Observing the rules on p. 8, write a thesis statement for each of the following topics:

1. American morals

2. Divorce

3. Rock and roll music

4. Student government

5. Sports cars

6. Pop art

7. Mercy killing

8. Bumper stickers

9. Television commercials

10. Diets

11. Tennis (or any other sport)

12. Draft laws

13. Planned parenthood

14. Boys' hair styles

15. A medical problem

Step 2. Enlarging the Pattern

The Informal Outline

Once you have committed to paper a well-expressed thesis statement, you will find that that old bugaboo, the outline, is far less likely to haunt you. In fact, as you start thinking about your thesis, you may start jotting down a few rough ideas to be included in your paper, not realizing that you are preparing an informal outline. But to be very useful to you these notes should not only indicate all the ideas you want to include in your paper but should also provide guidelines for breaking the material into paragraphs.

Let's say, for instance, that you have adopted as your thesis statement the following: *For most Americans religion today fills a social rather than a spiritual need.* In trying to decide why and how your thesis is true, you think about the people you know who attend church regularly. Not one of them can discuss the Bible in terms of history or philosophy, but if they continue to go to church they must get some satisfaction from it. What kind of satisfaction? Fran Pinkley gets personal fulfillment from singing with the church choir. Mary Lynn Rogers, who wants to be a teacher some day, enjoys helping the young children in her Sunday School class. Nils Larson gets satisfaction from the scouting program and the activities with the church youth group. And so on. You set down your ideas and examples, and soon you have far more than you need for a 500-word theme. Now you must decide which ideas are the most important, which stories are the most interesting. You want only four points (which can be expanded into four paragraphs) plus your introductory thesis. You arrange your illustrations in order of importance, saving the best one until last. And before you realize it, your informal outline has almost written itself.

Such an informal outline is all that is necessary for most English themes of 300-500 words. You needn't fret about the complex divisions and subdivisions which you probably think of in connection with the word *outline.* Nor must you struggle with parallel grammatical constructions. An informal outline requires only the following:

1. A well-expressed thesis statement which you will incorporate into the introductory paragraph. (*Now it is called a thesis.*)
2. 3-4 brief notes of sufficient importance to be expanded into 3-4 additional paragraphs of approximately 100 words each.

Below are two student themes which resulted from the same exercise where the teacher supplied an informal outline and asked the students to fill in the details.

Listening at Last

Thesis statement:
Dr. Landmann
has influenced
my life.

When I met Dr. Lewis C. Landmann, a balding Chicago dentist who has influenced my life greatly, I was smart, tough, and fifteen. I was also in trouble. I had "borrowed" a neighbor's car for a joy ride and had done a pretty good job of smashing in both it and my face. Now in my teens, I was a real mess to look at and would have to spend months and months while doctors and dentists put me back together again.

My first impression
of Dr. Landmann.

At fifteen, I guess I had never done much listening to adults. Dad had always been off bowling or golfing, so I had never had to listen to him. Whenever Mom said anything, I would either interrupt or grunt and walk away. But Dr. Landmann was something else. He invited me to sit down in his big black leather chair and relax my head on the back rest. Then just when I thought I could close my eyes and go to sleep, he jacked my mouth open with cotton wads, plastic wedges, steel tubes, rubber hoses—anything he could lay his hands on—and started to talk. I was trapped. Over the sounds of his drill and my own heavy breathing, I could still hear that boring Dr. Landmann talk.

An incident which reveals Dr. Landmann's character.

For the first visit or two he talked mostly about going to dental school in Seattle and about the rainy weather there. But one day he said, "I guess it wasn't worth it, was it?" I couldn't answer because of all the cotton wads and things, but I knew he was talking about my accident. "Ever notice this scar over my eye?" he went on. "I was in an accident when I was your age." Right then I realized that Dr. Landmann had been wanting to say something to me and had waited all this time until he thought I was ready to listen.

How Dr. Landmann has changed my thinking.

Finally having reached that point where I could listen, I learned many things from Dr. Landmann. I learned that being grown up means planning for tomorrow instead of grabbing every phony bit of happiness today. I learned that wisdom means profiting from the mistakes of others instead of entering every possible mistake on my own ledger. But most of all I learned that satisfaction means studying hard to become a dentist so that some day when the right fool kid comes along, I can jack his mouth open with cotton and steel and rubber—and start talking.

Notice how skillfully the student has molded his material to fit the teacher's assigned outline.

Thesis statement:
_____
has influenced my life.

The student introduces the influential character, showing also the kind of person the writer was himself as a teenager. But the student withholds HOW Dr. Landmann changed his life until the final paragraph. This technique not only conforms to the teacher's out-

	line but also maintains some slight suspense throughout the paper.
My first impression of_____.	The student remembers that as a teenager he never listened to adults and was never impressed by any of them at first. But circumstances compelled him to listen to Dr. Landmann.
An incident which reveals _____'s character.	The student recollects his hostility toward all adults and his surprise at discovering Dr. Landmann to be human after all.
How _____ has changed my thinking.	The student now answers the important question HOW: Dr. Landmann has changed his life by inspiring worthwhile goals.

So by thinking through the teacher's suggestions and closely adhering to the outline, the student has produced a successful theme. Part of his success, however, results from an element of his own: the transitions he has provided to link the separate paragraphs together.

Paragraph 2	"At fifteen" ties this paragraph to preceding one in which the student says he had been fifteen when he met Dr. Landmann. The conscious repetition provides a link between the two paragraphs.
Paragraph 3	The words "he talked" consciously repeat the idea "Dr. Landmann talk" from the end of the preceding paragraph.
Paragraph 4	The concept "where I could listen" again ties this paragraph to the preceding paragraph which ends, "I was ready to listen."

Conscious repetition of words, phrases, and concepts is only one transitional device. Others are discussed on p. 50. The important thing is that the student recognized that no matter how well the teacher planned the informal outline, more was necessary to make it successful.

The writer of the next theme also provides skillful transitions. See if you can find them as you read it. Although this paper is written about a different individual and the tone is considerably different from the one about Dr. Landmann, this student also carefully followed the teacher's informal outline.

Gregory

Thesis statement: Gregory has influenced my life.

Gregory is thirty-eight pounds worth of freckles, noise, grime, and trouble, and I haven't been the same since the day he came crashing into my life.

My first impression of Gregory.

That crash was literal, by the way. Gregory had been on the other end of a brick that came hurtling through our living room window the day we moved into our new home. Mother and Dad were off somewhere with the truck, and I was putting dishes away in the kitchen when a noise like three megatons of exploding hydrogen shook the floor boards. I rushed into the living room and through a hole in the window as big as his head I could see a boy in dirty blue jeans standing in the driveway. He took one look at me and streaked up the hill, so I rushed out the door in pursuit. He was faster than I had anticipated, and we had gone two blocks before I caught him. By then we were both panting, and my side ached. I was trying to find the breath to shake him or yell at him or whack his appropriate end when he looked up at me through a thatch of brown bangs. "Hi," he said with a grin. "I've been trying to meet you."

An incident which reveals Gregory's character.

Since then my life has been a series of skate boards in the driveway, sprinklers turned on at the wrong moments, blouses unpinned from the clothesline, lizards uncaged in my bedroom, and banana peelings left to rot in my car—all in the spirit of friendship and impish good humor. But one incident stands out more colorfully than the rest. It was about 8:15 a.m., and I was doing some last-minute cramming for Geology 13. Gregory came bursting through the door (he seldom knocks) crying "Marci, Marci, Gaylord has been murdered!" I dropped my book and ran outside to find my dog lying on the grass. He was alive all right, and not even whimpering, but he was covered with blood which of course I got all over my new skirt as I bent over to comfort him. Too late I noticed that the "blood" was the wrong shade of red, smelled like paint, and was splattered on the tip of Gregory's stubby nose.

How Gregory has changed my thinking.

Gregory's stubby nose has been in my life for nearly eight months now, and I am looking forward to graduation when I can get away from home and little boys. I once thought that I would like to marry and become the mother of an assortment of children of all ages and sexes. But Gregory has taught me that I can raise petunias, prim little girls, and possibly even lizards—but never anything resembling thirty-eight pounds worth of freckles, noise, grime, and trouble.

Two further things should be noted about these themes. In the first place, both of them rely heavily on narrative (or story) technique, but basically they are expository papers because in both themes the stories are used to explain the underlying ideas: *Dr. Landmann has influenced my life* and *Gregory has influenced my life*. In the second place, because these themes are expository, the paragraphs are fairly long—probably longer than you are used to writing. It is, of course, possible to write paragraphs which are disunified and too long. But the writer who prepares an informal outline ahead of time will seldom make this mistake. Nearly all writers, however, are occasionally tempted to write paragraphs which are brief and underdeveloped. Except for the shorter introduction (and the conclusion if there is one), expository paragraphs should average at least 100 words.

The Formal Outline

The formal outline is a more detailed pattern than the informal one and therefore provides the detailed assistance which you will need for long or technical papers. But it poses problems, too. For one thing, a formal outline requires logical thought, and its preparation may frighten you. For another thing, once you have prepared an outline, you may feel obliged to use it whether it proves workable or not. You should never hesitate to revise thoughtfully at any stage of composition. But you must remember that careful revision and careless inattention are reams of gobbledegook apart.

Formal outlines are of two types—the topic outline and the sentence outline. Certain rules apply to both.

1. Headings and subdivisions call for symbols as shown, evenly indented.

  I. Battle of Gettysburg
    A. Soldier
      1. Plup
      2. Men
        a. Shock
        b.
          (1)
          (2)
            (a)
            (b)
    B.
      1.
      2.
        a.
        b.
          (1)
          (2)
            (a)
            (b)

2. Capitalization and punctuation should be consistent.
   The first word of every entry is capitalized.
   All symbols and all sentences call for terminal punctuation.
   The use of periods after entries in a topic outline is optional
   but must be consistent.

3. Divisions must be logical.
   Entries must not overlap each other and must show proper
   division.

Overlapping Entries	Improved Entries
I. Kinds of fruit	I. Kinds of fruit
A. Apples	A. Apples
B. Bananas	B. Bananas
C. Citrus fruit	C. Oranges
D. Oranges	

Improper Division	Improved Division
I. Kinds of cars	I. Kinds of vehicles
A. Foreign cars	A. Foreign
B. American cars	1. Cars
C. Trucks	2. Trucks
	B. American
	1. Cars
	2. Trucks

4. Single subheadings are undesirable and illogical since nothing
   can be divided to make 1.

Single Subheading	No Subheading
I. His training	I. His training on the
A. On the Broadway	Broadway stage.
stage	II. His introduction to
II. His introduction to	Hollywood
Hollywood	

A fifth rule applies only to the topic outline since the sentence outline is always written in complete sentences:

5. Equal headings and subheadings call for parallel form.

Faulty Parallelism	Improved Parallelism
I. The value of good reading	I. The value of good reading
A. For children	A. For children
1. Stimulates the imagination	1. Stimulates the imagination
2. Good study habits	2. Develops good study habits
B. As an adult	B. For adults
1. To broaden horizons	1. To broaden their horizons
2. Lonely hours	2. To occupy their lonely hours
3. Understanding others	3. To increase their understanding of others
II. How to set up a home library	II. A suggestion for setting up a home library

Before you submit a difficult research paper, your teacher may wish to review your outline for the project. Although at first this may seem like an unnecessary extra assignment, you will probably find that your teacher's suggestions will save many hours of valuable writing time. Such an outline prepared for someone else to read should be as complete as possible and therefore consist of (1) title, (2) thesis statement, and (3) sentence entries.

A detailed sentence outline will also prove useful for any composition that you cannot attend to shortly. After several days or weeks the cold, abbreviated entries of a topic outline may lose their meaning.

But neither kind of formal outline—topic or sentence—will be considered further in this book. Our purposes here are to study methods for non-technical writing, and Steps 3 through 9 will be structured on the informal outline discussed above.

Exercises

A. Theme Assignment

Write a theme of 300-500 words based on the informal outline below. Compose an original title.

1st paragraph: _____ has influenced my life. (Thesis)

2nd paragraph: My first impression of _____.

3rd paragraph: An incident which reveals _____'s character.

4th paragraph: How _____ has changed my thinking.

B. Informal Outline

Write a thesis statement and an informal outline for each of the following topics:

Salesmanship

_____

_____

_____

_____

_____

_____

_____

_____

LSD

_____

_____

_____

_____

_____

_____

_____

_____

Riots

_____

_____

_____

_____

_____

_____

_____

_____

Step 3. Perfecting the Pattern

Having prepared your informal outline, you may begin to worry about how to translate those rough notes into a finished paper. Probably it will help you if you will pause for a moment to think briefly about three things:

How should the paper begin?

How should the paper end?

How will the ideas hang together?

It is not really necessary to set down the answers to these questions, but you will find it helpful to have some overall view of where your theme is headed and how.

How Should the Paper Begin?

By definition, an introduction should *introduce* a composition—both its subject matter and its tone. (For a discussion of tone, see Postscript, p.170.) Most students realize the importance of a good introduction. But often in their anxiety to say something clever or profound they will struggle with beginnings which are self-conscious, overblown, painfully obvious, or weakening to the general structure of the paper. The irony is that all of these problems could be avoided if the writer would stop fighting his material and let it work for him—with a thesis beginning.

Good Introductions: Thesis Beginnings

1. *The first-sentence thesis.*

Until you gain confidence as a writer, you should always state your thesis as soon as possible within an expository composition because if you are attentive to it, it will provide a pattern for the paper and help guard against irrelevant material. Moreover, by using that thesis as your very first sentence, you not only solve that how-do-I-begin problem but also provide a first sentence which is clear, direct, and interesting. (If the thesis isn't interesting, your paper can't possibly be so, and you might as well throw it out right now.)

Although few Americans can discuss the role of Horace Mann in their national history, they cannot escape his influence.

It is a successful mother lion who raises one out of a litter of four cubs, for young lions have many natural enemies.

By breaking the thesis into two or three elements, you can construct an even more useful design.

American women are more aggressive, more selfish, and more unhappy than European women.

The outcome of the Civil War might have been different if the Southern troops had been provided with better supply lines and more practical distribution of the foodstuffs at hand.

2. *A question which leads directly to the thesis.*

A question often attracts the eye more quickly than a declaration and therefore may be successfully used as an introduction to a piece of exposition. Because the beginner is apt to ask empty questions (see Poor Introductions on p. 28), you will find it safer to limit yourself to the question which can be answered in the next sentence by the thesis.

Are all crocodiles as dangerous to man as commonly supposed? The small crocodiles in Lake Baringo have never been known to harm a human although natives wade constantly in the fish-filled water.

How do you develop a child's creativity? Give him simple tools—blackboards, blocks, tablets of plain paper—not coloring books and fancy mechanical toys.

3. A contrast which emphasizes the thesis.

The underlying idea of your paper may be heightened by contrasting it with circumstances of another time or situation.

> As we drive through the uncluttered regions of Kansas, Nebraska, Wyoming, Utah, and Nevada, we wonder about all the concern over population explosion. The little country of Israel, however, presents another picture.

> In our anxiety about the toll of human lives from plane crashes in this air age, we sometimes overlook the magnitude of the sea disasters such as the one of April 15, 1912, which claimed nearly 1,500 persons.

Good Introductions: Delayed Theses (For Advanced Student Writers)

No doubt the time will come when the three thesis beginnings listed above will no longer challenge you, and you will want to try other possibilities. And of course you realize already that good exposition can begin in a wide variety of ways. But any introduction which delays the thesis beyond the first paragraph poses risks for the inexperienced writer because (1) he loses the obvious sign-post which keeps him on course, and (2) he may even accidentally insert a second thesis which widens the focus of his paper or contradicts his underlying idea. Therefore, if you want to experiment with one of the additional good introductions listed here, you should still try to state your thesis for the reader (and for yourself) within the first or second paragraph.

4. A statement designed to startle the reader.

A sentence which surprises the reader with frank or unusual information can often attract attention for the soon-to-follow presentation of a thesis.

> I probably hold the world's record for the number of times anyone has ever taken beginning swimming.

> The followers of Ann Lee believed that she was literally the Messiah, who had come to earth in the form of a woman.

> My car hates me.

5. *A brief dramatic incident.*

A brief incident or story may provide a dramatic beginning for a paper. But in writing exposition you should remember that your main purpose is to explain an idea, not to tell a story. Therefore, of all the good introductions included here, this one poses the most risks.

> A great flash of light cut from east to west across the Hiroshima sky.

> Every morning red-haired Lennie Bills walks three miles down a dirt road with his seeing-eye dog, Minx.

> The woman stood gray and silent as rescue workers lowered the doctor down the shaft of the old mine.

6. *A statement which relates the subject to a topic of current interest.*

Even a topic of limited historical interest can be made meaningful by relating it to a problem of more immediate concern.

> It might be argued that not God but William McGuffey was excluded from the American classroom when the Supreme Court ruled that prescribed prayers were unconstitutional.

7. *A statement which anticipates the reader's possible objections.*

Argumentative writing may call for a comment which disarms possible critics.

> Those of us who have been amused by "Fenimore Cooper's Literary Offenses" by Mark Twain have perhaps never looked at Natty Bumppo seriously. Nevertheless, *The Deerslayer* is clearly worthy of more than mere ridicule.

8. *A quotation.*

When all else fails, you can always borrow a striking quotation, preferably from someone who is an authority on the subject about which he is speaking. Credit, of course, must be given.

> "It is far better to let a beast get away unwounded," warns White Hunter Donald Ker, "than to chance a wild shot."

These eight suggestions for good introductions are only a start. You will discover many more as you gain confidence and experience. But practicing with these eight good beginnings should keep anyone too busy to resort to the tedious openers listed below.

Poor Introductions: Beginnings That Fail to Begin

1. *The apology.*

I don't know very much about barracks life because I have never been in the Army, but . . .

I wanted to write a paper on X-Ray techniques in World War I, but the librarian . . .

2. *The echo of the title.*

THE SINISTER BLACK WIDOW SPIDER

The sinister black widow spider is . . .

WHAT GEORGE WASHINGTON MEANS TO TWENTIETH CENTURY AMERICANS

What George Washington means to twentieth century Americans can be summed up . . .

3. *The sentence that depends upon the title to be understood.*

LOVE

This is a word which stirs up . . .

TERMITES

Whenever a person sees one of these creatures, he . . .

Both problems of numbers 2 and 3 can easily be avoided by delaying the composition of a title until the theme is completed. You will also find it easier to write a more appropriate title after the paper is finished.

4. *The dictionary definition.* (Not to be confused with the extended definition discussed in Step 9.)

Before talking about *homemaking,* let us turn to the dictionary to see . . .

According to Webster, *patriotism* is . . .

5. *The Much Ado About Nothing* or important-sounding declaration of a commonplace idea.

Ever since the dawn of history, proud mothers and fathers have fought back tears of joy as their children . . .

6. *The meaningless question for which there is no answer.*

What little girl has not at one time or another wondered about the prince charming who . . .

Who in his lifetime has never done something that he was not sorry for . . .

7. *The formal declaration of the paper's purpose.*
   In this paper I shall discuss . . .

In general, your writing will come off much better if you don't struggle to begin with something unusual but merely **begin.** Many students will strain to convert a dull, empty statement into something clever at the same time that they bury a straightforward and well-expressed thesis in the second paragraph—or beyond. Check for such a possibility the next time your first page just doesn't seem to move.

Another possibility—perhaps even more important—is that you are struggling with a subject in which you as a writer are not interested. Certainly you will never engage a reader with a title, an introduction, or any part of a paper dealing with a topic which does not completely involve **you.**

How Should the Paper End?

Although some writers and readers have difficulty accepting the notion, *not every piece of exposition calls for a formal conclusion.* A *good* conclusion is always appropriate, of course. However, a short, simple theme with no formal ending will not seem to halt abruptly if (1) you have fully developed your thesis and (2) you have been careful to place the most important paragraph last. The kind of ending which merely repeats the beginning or summarizes the whole is very useful in a long or technical paper. But for most of the short themes you will write in your English classes, such a conclusion is as wilted and colorless as last week's cut flowers.

But despite what has been said here, you may still feel uncomfortable without a formal conclusion. Certainly the experience gained in writing conclusions for short themes will be useful when the time comes for longer and more difficult papers. For either a long or short paper one of the five endings listed below will always be appropriate:

1. *A significant quotation which supports the thesis.*

And so we agree with Emerson: "Every great and commanding moment in the annals of the world is the triumph of some enthusiasm."

2. *An anecdote, or story, which illustrates the thesis.*

In moments like these I think back to old, stooped Wilford Kaiser, the "nutty guy" who lived down the street when I was a boy. With his straw hat pushed back on his head and his suspenders holding up a baggy pair of brown pants, he knelt each day in the vacant lot next to his home because even though he didn't own it, he couldn't bear to see anything "go to weeds."

3. *A solution for a problem presented in the paper.*

Countries, like parents, may find that greater cooperation comes from fewer challenges to the sense of importance and self-esteem.

4. *A statement designed to make the reader think about or act upon the problem suggested by the paper.*

If a man cares enough about his wife to reduce the years she must spend in lonely isolation as a widow, he will pay closer attention to his eating habits and physical activities.

5. *A memorable restatement of the thesis through the use of figures of speech, emphasis, balance, or other qualities of distinctive prose discussed in Part III of this book.*

. . . and that government of the people, by the people, for the people, shall not perish from the earth.

Lincoln "Gettysburg Address"

Or for a long paper you may use the more familiar ending:

6. *A summary of the major points in the composition.*

Thus an examination of the newspaper writings of Mark Twain reveals little journalistic merit. The climaxes are misplaced. The insults are abusive. The humor is generally strained. Nevertheless, the articles are important historically because they evidence techniques which he would later develop and master.

One word of caution: A good conclusion must always follow logically from the information which precedes it in the paper. Never should you use a conclusion to introduce new material which you were not able to discuss in the theme.

How Will the Ideas Hang Together

The paragraphs of a piece of exposition are something like the single beads of a necklace. A cord holds the beads together, but seldom—if the beads are well strung—can it be seen. In the same way, something must hold the paragraphs together, but that something should not be too obvious. The composition as a whole should occupy the reader's attention.

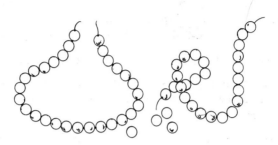

When writing holds together well, it is said to cohere, which literally means "to stick." Coherence is achieved by

1. The logical arrangement of ideas so that one leads naturally to the next.

2. The use of transitions. (Words, phrases, sentences, or even paragraphs that act as bridges between different ideas.)

Both elements are necessary and must work together. Transitional devices alone cannot hold a theme together if the ideas have not been thoughtfully arranged. And without transitional devices the most carefully laid out prose will jerk and hop about like the sentences in a first-grade primer:

> As late as the early 1800's there were no free schools in America. In the west there was very little education. Parents knew some schooling was useful. A boy should figure well enough to barter his fox and marten pelts for a fair price. A girl should be able to sound out Biblical passages. There was little else to do on a frontier evening but to sit as a family with the scriptures. Most of the parents provided a month or two of education at one of the subscription schools. The necessities of rural life—land to be cleared, lead balls to be cast for the rifles, flax to be carded and spun—allowed no time for scholarship.

The words added to the following paragraph do not change the meaning, but they clarify the meaning by providing useful links between ideas:

As late as the early 1800's there were no free schools in America *and at least* in the west, very little education *at all*. Parents knew schooling was useful, *of course*. A boy should figure well enough to barter his fox and marten pelts for a fair price. A girl should be able to sound out Biblical passages, *for* there was little else to do on a frontier evening but to sit as a family with the scriptures. Most of the parents *therefore* provided some education—a month or two *anyway*—at one of the subscription schools. *But* the necessities of rural life—land to be cleared, lead balls to be cast for the rifles, flax to be carded and spun—allowed no time for scholarship.

Although clarity is the primary aim of exposition, a writer should strive to achieve it through means other than wordiness and obvious transitions. Transitional devices like "Let us turn now to the next point" call unnecessary attention to themselves but are usually better than no transitions at all.

In the same way, some theses seem to lead to mechanical systems for numbering paragraphs:

thesis:

> The college graduate who has worked on the campus newspaper has at least four advantages over some of his classmates.

2nd paragraph:

> In the first place, he has trained himself to be observant . . .

3rd paragraph:

> In the second place, he has learned to converse with strangers . . .

4th paragraph:

> In the third place, he has acquired the skill of expressing himself . . .

5th paragraph:

> In the fourth place, he has become more aware of what is going on in the world . . .

Such a treatment is both clear and orderly. But it leaves little to the reader's imagination and is therefore dull, particularly to someone (like an English teacher) who must read many papers constructed the same way. With a little effort the writer can incorporate the transitions into the prose:

thesis:	The college graduate who has worked on the campus newspaper has at least four advantages over some of his classmates.
2nd paragraph:	One advantage is that he has trained himself to be observant . . .
3rd paragraph:	In addition, he has learned to converse with strangers . . .
4th paragraph:	He has also acquired the skill of expressing himself . . .
5th paragraph:	But probably the most important advantage is that he has become more aware of what is going on in the world.

The specific transitional devices which hold a paragraph together (see p. 50) will also lend coherence to a theme. But there are additional devices which work effectively in a larger piece of writing:

1. Use of short transitional paragraphs (see Step 4).
2. Use of a final sentence in a paragraph which suggests the next topic idea.
3. Use of a beginning sentence in a paragraph which refers back to the final sentence or topic idea of preceding paragraph.
4. Use of a sustained comparison throughout the paper (*e.g.,* comparison of an Indian's preparation for battle with an artist's preparation to paint).

In addition, tight methods of organization which permit little variation (such as time order and space order) lend greater coherence than do loose methods of organization, but these methods are seldom used throughout a long composition (see Step 5).

Exercises

A. Good Introductions

Write an introduction for a theme based on each of the following thesis statements:

1. Every parent has a responsibility to give his child _____. (Use Good Introduction 1, and break the thesis into three elements.)

2. Maturity is measured by _____. (Use Good Introduction 1, and break the thesis into three elements.)

3. Life in American suburbs is _____. (Use Good Introduction 2, and begin with a question.)

4. People can overcome loneliness by _____. (Use Good Introduction 2, and begin with a question.)

5. Teenagers have many problems. (Use Good Introduction 3, and contrast the thesis with circumstances of another time or situation.)

6. _____ is a dangerous hobby. (Use Good Introduction 4, and begin with frank or startling information.)

7. _____ is a dangerous hobby. (Use Good Introduction 5, and begin with brief incident or story.)

8. Some people love animals more than they love other people. (Use Good Introduction 5, and begin with a brief incident or story.)

9. Americans are ridiculous. (Use Good Introduction 8, and begin with a quotation.)

10. Medical science has not solved _____. (Use Good Introduction 8, and begin with a quotation.)

B. Emphatic Arrangement

When a writer fails to provide a formal conclusion for his composition, he should arrange his paragraphs in ascending order with the most important point at the end. Re-arrange the following entries so that the most important one comes last.

    A. Automobiles have helped (hindered) life in America since 1900. (Thesis)
    B. Moral values.
    C. Health values.
    D. Economic and practical values.
    E. Esthetic values.

A. Automobiles have helped (hindered) life in America since 1900. (Thesis)

B. _____

C. _____

D. _____

E. _____

Checklist for Patterns

☐ 1. Is my thesis statement clear?
☐ 2. Does it focus on a narrow aspect of the topic?
☐ 3. Does it set forth my point of view?
☐ 4. Is it expressed in a complete sentence (not a question)?
☐ 5. Is it an unusual statement worthy of examination?
☐ 6. Have I planned an introduction that will interest the reader?
☐ 7. If I haven't used a thesis beginning, have I planned for the setting down of my thesis within the first or second paragraph?
☐ 8. Does my rough outline provide 3 or 4 brief entries of sufficient importance to be expanded into 3 or 4 additional paragraphs of at least 100 words each?
☐ 9. Do the entries of my rough outline follow a logical sequence that will help my paper hang together?
☐ 10. Have I arranged the material so that the paper will conclude with the most significant point (especially if I have not planned for a formal conclusion)?
☐ 11. If I plan to use a formal conclusion, will it be one that leaves a good impression?
☐ 12. Is my subject one in which I am genuinely interested?

PART II

Giving Your Paragraphs Substance

Step 4. Letting the Topic Sentence Help You

A topic sentence is one which summarizes the content of the paragraph in one concise statement. It therefore functions within a paragraph in the same way that a thesis functions within a larger composition such as a theme or a term paper.

The Paragraph	The Whole Composition
1. Develops a single, fairly simple idea	1. Develops a single, more thoughtful idea
2. May contain a *topic sentence,* which summarizes the idea of the paragraph for the reader	2. May contain a *thesis,* which summarizes the idea of the whole composition for the reader

Although you may place the topic sentence anywhere within a paragraph, you will probably find that a topic sentence placed at the beginning will help you write a better paragraph. Like the carefully-worded thesis at the beginning of a theme, the clearly-stated topic sentence at the first of a paragraph will serve as a pattern which helps you focus your material so you won't be tempted to set down any distracting ideas. Thus, the topic sentence, when wisely followed, can be extremely useful.

Nevertheless, beginners often write topic sentences that try to cover too much. Of course any topic sentence is a general statement, but it should focus on one small aspect of a problem. A good topic sentence therefore not only summarizes the whole paragraph, but it also contains special *key words* or clues. These key words represent the *controlling idea* because they control what part of the topic sentence you must emphasize in the paragraph.

The topic sentence in the paragraph below talks about weapons, enemies, and Alaskan Indians. A careless writer might try to introduce material about any of these in his paragraph. But the student who wrote the paragraph has limited his supporting material to the controlling idea expressed in the key words *wars of gift-giving*.

> Instead of taking up weapons against their enemies, certain clans of Alaskan Indians engage in wars of gift giving. To huge feasts—called *potlatches*—the hosts and guests will bring their most valuable belongings. Fur blankets, canoes, copper shields and slaves may change hands as each clan tries to outgive the other. Much food is wasted, and some gifts are destroyed by fire to add to the show. By imposing unbearable shame upon its enemy, the clan which offers the most valuable gifts wins the contest without the unnecessary shedding of blood.

The three student paragraphs below illustrate wise and careless use of topic sentences. Paragraph A is poor because it contains no controlling idea, a guidepost which the writer obviously needs. Paragraph B is poor because although it contains a satisfactory controlling idea, the student ignores it as he develops the paragraph. Paragraph C is a good one in which key words carefully control the development.

Paragraph A	Poor—No controlling idea
Water skiing is my favorite sport. Last summer we took a trailer to Lake Tahoe and discovered a cove where the water is shallow and not very cold. A professional instructor from Florida was there, and he used no skis at all but skimmed across the water on the soles of his feet. He tried to teach me how to get up on only one ski. I have not yet mastered the art, but I am learning. In winter I also enjoy zooming	"Water skiing is my favorite sport" would make a fair thesis statement for an entire theme, but it is too large an idea to serve as the topic sentence for a paragraph. It needs to be focused more sharply through the use of a controlling idea, or key words, such as "I enjoy the *physical challenge* of water skiing." Because the student lacks a narrow idea to focus on, he tries to tell us everything he knows about water skiing in one paragraph. The individual sentences are not bad, but they cannot be put together this way without creating a disunified paragraph. Even the material

down a mountain on snow skis and feeling the sting of wind in my face.

about the trip to Lake Tahoe might be divided into several well-unified paragraphs. Of course, the comment about snow skiing has nothing at all to do with why water skiing is the student's favorite sport and should be eliminated.

Paragraph B

My dog causes lots of trouble for the people in our neighborhood. The neighbors don't like him because of all the things he does. Some people say I should either keep him tied up or get rid of him. I don't want to do either of those things because I love dogs. If I should keep him tied up, I suppose he might not get into so much trouble, but that doesn't sound like a good way to treat a dog. I think dogs should be allowed to roam just like people. This is a free country, isn't it?

Poor—Unheeded controlling idea

The topic sentence contains a controlling idea—*trouble*—but instead of focusing on what kind of trouble the dog causes, the student introduces a new problem: whether or not the dog should be tied up. The paragraph is also needlessly wordy, using two sentences to state the topic idea when one well-written one would do a better job. The next three sentences could also be combined into one. In addition, the last sentence represents the unreasonable kind of argument which emotional and unthinking people sometimes use. The United States Constitution says nothing about dogs, so the statement is of course not logical.

Paragraph C

Of all the birds of sea and sand the albatross is the largest and the most graceful. Looking like a giant gull, he stands about three feet tall and stretches his wings to more than eleven feet. These long, slender wings help him soar for periods of time exceeded by no other bird. Without a single flutter he glides for miles, sometimes so near the water

Good—Clear controlling idea

This paragraph is well developed because the student has heeded the key words in the topic sentence: *largest* and *most graceful*. The second sentence provides specific information to show that the bird is large. The third sentence is a careful transition which moves from the idea of large to the idea of graceful. The student repeats the word *wings*, but this time also uses the word *slender* to describe them. The last sentence describes in a concrete way the bird's graceful motion in flight. Notice

that he completely vanishes
behind the rising peaks of
ocean.

how the key words—largest and most
graceful—have been developed in the
paragraph in the same order that they
appear in the topic sentence.

WHEN TO MOVE THE TOPIC SENTENCE

Even though as a rule you should introduce each main paragraph with a topic sentence, you may choose to vary this method occasionally in order to keep the prose flowing smoothly. Sometimes a transition sentence will be necessary at the beginning, in which case you can move the topic sentence to the second position in the paragraph.

Transition sentence

Topic sentence

Illustration

But hair is not the only part of the body to which savages attach strange customs. *Many primitive people believe that special care must be taken to prevent the soul from leaving the mouth when one is eating or drinking.* Certain natives of the Slave Coast, for instance, fear that not only may a man's own soul depart while he is eating but that a homeless and unwelcome spirit may take the opportunity to enter his body. For this reason they bar their houses while they eat so that their spirits may not stray far from their bodies.

Although there are many other ways to construct an expository paragraph, you will probably find that until you have mastered all twelve steps in this book you should begin each paragraph with (1) a topic sentence or (2) a transition sentence followed by a topic sentence.

PARAGRAPH LENGTH

Often a newspaper story giving a long list of names—for instance the names of new members of a college fraternity—will break the list into several paragraphs. A newspaper is printed in columns of four or five words across. In order to make each page attractive to the eye and easy to read, typesetters break material into small units. Newspaper paragraphs are seldom more than one or two sentences, and long lists are printed in several paragraphs.

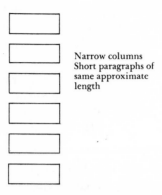

Narrow columns
Short paragraphs of
same approximate
length

Newspaper Stories

The writer of short stories and novels has more freedom in the length of paragraphs he writes. His paragraphs may be long or short, depending upon the effect he is trying to create. Long paragraphs tend to slow down the action of the story. Short paragraphs hurry the pace.

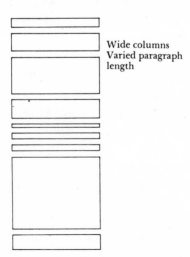

Wide columns
Varied paragraph
length

Fiction

But what about the paragraphs for your college themes and term papers? *Every paragraph in exposition develops a sharply-focused idea.* And over the years good and bad writers have shown us about how many words and sentences are required to develop an idea properly. Naturally, complicated ideas call for more words than simple ones. But most undergraduate papers discuss fairly simple ideas in fairly short sentences. *Four to eight sentences per paragraph are generally required.*

In your anxiety to get to the end of a theme you may find yourself leaping across a page like a grasshopper over a barren field. But failing to light on an idea long enough really to look at it results in a string of general statements which are never fully developed. Because even the most simple expository idea cannot be developed in one, two, or even three sentences, you should pay careful attention to the length of your paragraphs. Short paragraphs should appear rarely and then only for specific reasons:

1. Transition
2. Summary
3. Emphasis or attention

1. *You may use a short paragraph for transition.* Between two long paragraphs on different subjects you may need to provide a transition or linking paragraph of some kind. For example, two separate paragraphs devoted first to Babe Ruth and then to Mickey Mantle may call for a one-sentence transition paragraph something like this:

> Another Yankee who has slugged his way into American hearts is Mickey Mantle.

2. *You may use a short paragraph for summary.* Between two similar paragraphs on Babe Ruth and Mickey Mantle you may prefer to make a brief summary about Ruth before introducing Mantle. Or perhaps you will write a brief paragraph which serves both purposes of summary and transition:

> After a lifetime of making baseball history, George Herman Ruth died of cancer in 1948. Mickey Mantle was sixteen years old at the time.

3. *You may use a short paragraph for emphasis or attention.* Obviously a very short paragraph coming between two longer ones will call attention to itself on the printed page. Such a paragraph is

therefore useful for the dramatic presentation of an idea you care to emphasize:

> At forty, when men in other professions are at the peaks of their careers, "The King of Swat" was too old for baseball.

Unless these short paragraphs are used sparingly for the purposes listed here, they lose their effectiveness and become merely brief, underdeveloped units. In a theme of 500 words the introductory paragraph need not be long, but you should not use more than one other short paragraph of fewer than four sentences. The remaining paragraphs should all be approximately the same length—that is, long enough to develop their topic sentences thoroughly.

Wide columns
Main paragraphs
approximately 100-150 words

Exposition

PARAGRAPH UNITY

In exposition the paragraph is the smallest unit of thought which develops an idea. Words and sentences can talk about ideas, but they cannot develop them. Nor can a paragraph develop an idea if that idea is too large, too vague, or too poorly expressed.

Whatever other qualities they possess, expository paragraphs must be unified—that is, each paragraph must develop one idea and one idea only. To help achieve that necessary paragraph unity, you will find these rules helpful:

1. Begin each main paragraph with a topic sentence or a transition sentence followed by a topic sentence.

2. Focus the topic sentence on one aspect of a problem by means of key words (controlling idea).

3. Develop the controlling idea in from four to seven additional (and concrete) sentences.

4. Use short paragraphs of one, two, or three sentences sparingly and only for transition, summary, or emphasis.

Steps 6 through 9 of this book will explain rule 3 above in detail, showing how you develop paragraphs by means of detail, illustration, comparison and contrast, analysis, definition, and reasons. It is unlikely that any single expository paper will use all of these methods of development, or even most of them. But in order to write varied and convincing prose, you must become aware of the urgency of giving your paragraphs substance and the methods by which you may do so.

Paragraph Coherence

Although unity is the single most important quality of any expository paragraph, it is quite possible for a paragraph to be unified without flowing smoothly from one sentence to the next. Within the paragraph as within the entire theme, coherence (or the quality of hanging together properly) is dependent upon (1) the logical arrangement of material, and (2) the use of transitional devices. The most common transitional devices are as follows:

1. Transitional words and phrases
2. Repetition of key terms
3. Synonyms and other substitutes
4. Pronouns
5. Parallel constructions

1. *Transitional words and phrases.* Conjunctions are the least formal of the transitional words and phrases and seem the most natural in student writing. Despite the warning some high school English teacher may have given you about not beginning a sentence

with a coordinating conjunction, such words as *and* and *but* are now considered appropriate transitional devices in prose, particularly in the fairly informal themes which most students write. Other conjunctions commonly used for transitions are *for, yet, so,* and *nor* as well as such subordinating conjunctions as *before, although, when, after, since,* and *because.*

Conjunctive adverbs (also known as transitional connectives) are used less commonly in speech than simple conjunctions and sometimes seem forced when students try to incorporate them into their somewhat informal themes; but they do hold sentences together and lend smoothness to the flow of prose. Conjunctive adverbs include such words as *consequently, nevertheless, otherwise, however, therefore, indeed, moreover, furthermore,* and *accordingly.*

Some phrases add little meaning to a sentence but merely serve as links between ideas. Examples would include such expressions as *in other words, in addition, in the first place, in conclusion, to sum up, for example,* and *as a matter of fact.*

2. *Repetition of key terms.* Possibly you know someone who bores you beyond endurance because he is always repeating the same unfunny jokes. Or perhaps he repeats the same ideas and expressions until the mere sound of his voice is as irritating as the droning of a fly when you are trying desperately to sleep. But from situations such as these you should not conclude that all repetition is tasteless and unnecessary. Repetition of those key words which carry essential meaning is often useful in achieving clarity and coherence in prose:

> During the religious revival of the 1830's, many Americans were prophesying that the *second coming* of Christ was at hand. Based on personal visions and on passages from the Bible, at least sixty papers had been written on the subject by 1836. One earnest New England farmer, *William Miller,* traveled throughout the villages near his home, preaching that *Christ* would appear in 1843 on approximately the *twenty-first of March.* As *March 21* approached, Miller's followers—numbering more than 50,000—went outdoors and climbed hilltops to await the *second coming.* But the day brought only disappointment and a new statement by *Miller* that the event might occur any time that year. Still disappointed on March 21, 1844, the leaders set

an exact day: October 22, 1844. This time the Millerites were more confident than ever and waited in graveyards and atop roofs in their finest clothes. When the day passed quietly, most of the faithful still insisted that *Christ's coming* was at hand but refused to comment on the exact date.

3. *Synonyms and other substitutes.* To avoid the wooden-sounding prose resulting from constant repetition, a writer will often substitute synonyms and other expressions for key terms. Several examples can be shown from the previous paragraph.

key term	*substitutes*
prophesying	personal visions
	papers had been written
	preaching
	statement
	set
	insisted
second coming of Christ	the subject
	would appear
	the event
Miller's followers	the leaders
	the Millerites
	the faithful

Word substitutes must of course be natural and not call attention to themselves. Student themes which reach for synonyms like *duenna, coryphaeus, prelector, dominie, preceptor,* or *pedagogue* for the simple word *teacher,* for example, are both self-conscious and stilted.

4. *Pronouns.* Transitions between sentences also can be accomplished by the use of pronoun substitutes for key words:

> The gopher is a slow-moving American rodent *which* is slightly larger than a common house rat. A burrowing animal, *it* digs with the strong claws on *its* forefeet and *its* overhanging front teeth. The gopher is unable to see well and therefore frequently moves backward, using *its* tail as an organ of touch. *It* eats grass, nuts, roots, and farm produce which *it* carries in *its* cheek pouches. The gopher's burrow can be detected from aboveground because of the small mounds of dirt along the way.

The foregoing paragraph is a simple one in which all of the pronouns except the second *which* (not italicized in the text) refer back to the same antecedent—gopher—and the meaning is clear throughout.

Teachers are often reluctant to encourage students to use pronouns for transitions because inexperienced writers, as a rule, are inclined to use too many pronouns rather than too few and frequently commit grammatical errors in the process. Whenever you use a pronoun, therefore, you should consciously remind yourself of what antecedent (noun) that pronoun is standing in for.

5. *Parallelism.* The repetition of grammatical constructions not only lends rhythm and balance to prose (see p. 153) but also provides useful transitions.

> Probably no other American has distinguished himself in so many fields as has Benjamin Franklin. As a writer he edited a successful periodical and wrote hundreds of sayings which are common household expressions. As a scholar he established a circulating library, the American Philosophical Society, and an academy which later became the University of Pennsylvania. As a scientist and inventor he produced bi-focal glasses, a stove, and a harmonica and studied the properties of electricity. As a public servant he reorganized the postal system, making it efficient and profitable. As a statesman he helped with the Declaration of Independence, served in the Constitutional Convention, and ably represented this country in Britain and France. Indeed, he earned the title *the wisest American.*

In this paragraph the repetition of the beginning phrase "As a . . ." holds the material together and helps to give emphasis to the final idea.

Of course, failure to provide adequate transitions may occur at any place within a paper, but most frequently omissions occur where you are thinking about other things, such as providing examples for your generalizations. Be careful, then, to relate your examples or arguments to the points you are trying to make. The following paragraphs show a typical student error and how it was corrected.

Inadequate transitions	Corrected paragraph
If patience, coordination, and ambidexterity are among your humble skills, a world of hungry people is waiting. The job of waitressing is demanding	If patience, coordination, and ambidexterity are among your humble skills, a world of hungry people is waiting, *for you could become a skilled*

and, all too frequently, not rewarding. With determination
and the willingness to pursue
the trial-and-error method, the
following pattern will rise as
clearer water from the mud.

waitress. The job of waitressing
is demanding and, all too frequently, not rewarding. *But*
with determination and the
willingness to pursue the trial-
and-error method, the following pattern will rise as clearer
water from the mud.

Exercises

A. Paragraph Assignment

Using one of the subjects below, write a unified, coherent paragraph
of approximately 100-150 words which begins with a topic sentence.
Underline the controlling idea (key words) in the topic sentence.

1. A recommendation for my college president
2. A recommendation for my congressman
3. A critical analysis of a literary character
4. A critical analysis of an historical figure

B. Recognizing Transitional Devices

Underline all the transitional devices in the following paragraph and identify what kinds they are in the margin at the right.

Lincoln, nevertheless, rather than Jackson, was the supreme American of our history. In Clay, East and West were mixed without being fused or harmonized: he seems like two men. In Jackson there was not even a mixture; he was all of a piece, and altogether unacceptable to some parts of the country, —a frontier statesman. But in Lincoln the elements were combined and harmonized. The most singular thing about the wonderful career of the man is the way in which he steadily grew into a national stature. He began an amorphous, unlicked cub, bred in the rudest of human lairs; but, as he grew, everything formed, informed, transformed him. The process was slow but unbroken. He was not fit to be President until he actually became President. He was fit then because, learning everything as he went, he had found out how much there was to learn, and had still an infinite capacity for learning. The quiet voices of sentiment and murmurs of resolution that went through the land, his ear always caught, when others could hear nothing but their own words. He never ceased to be a common man: that was his source of strength. But he was a common man with genius, a genius for things American, for insight into the common thought, for mastery of the fundamental things of politics that inhere in human nature and cast hardly more than their shadows on constitutions; for the practical niceties of affairs; for judging men and assessing arguments. Jackson had no social imagination: no unfamiliar community made any impression on him. His whole fibre stiffened young, and nothing afterward could modify or even deeply affect it. But Lincoln was always a-making; he would have died unfinished if the terrible storms of the war had not stung him to learn in those four years what no other twenty could have taught him. And, as he stands there in his complete manhood, at the most perilous helm in Christendom, what a marvelous composite figure he is! The whole country is summed up in him: the rude Western strength, tempered with shrewdness and a broad and human wit; the Eastern conservatism, regardful of law and devoted to fixed standards of duty. He even understood the South, as no other Northern man of his generation did. He respected, because he comprehended, though he could not hold, its views of the Constitution; he appreciated the inexorable compulsions of its past in respect of slavery; he would have secured it once more, and speedily if possible, in its right to self-government, when the fight was fought out. To the Eastern politicians he seemed like an accident; but to history he must seem like a providence.

Woodrow Wilson "A Calendar of Great Americans" quoted in *Points of Departure* by Arthur J. Carr and William Steinhoff, Harper & Row, Publishers.

C. Supplying Transitional Devices

The following student theme is in need of transitional devices to link the ideas together. Provide whatever words, phrases, clauses, or sentences you feel are necessary.

A BIG DECISION

When I graduated from high school, I was faced with many decisions to make. I was married and worked only part time at a service station. I didn't know whether to go on to school, or go to work at Kennecott Copper, or even go into the service. I was so flustered I didn't know what I wanted to do.

All my family are college graduates and my two older brothers are attending the University of Utah. They all wanted me to go on to school and make something out of myself. My father said he would pay all my expenses if I decided to go to school. I didn't want my father to pay my way. I was on my own and couldn't depend on someone else to pay my way. I had to get along without help from my father.

I had a chance to get a high paying job working for Kennecott, but

I wouldn't be able to go to school. This job was very tempting, but I

wanted to look around before I decided.

I was also thinking seriously about going into the service. This thought

quickly vanished from my mind when I found out how much money I

would be making and the hours I would be away from my family.

I decided I would try to find a job that would enable me to go to

school and work full time. I spent many months looking for this kind

of job, and I finally found exactly what I was looking for. The job was

with Mountain Fuel Supply Company; it was a night job, from 3:00 to

12:00 midnight. The job paid very well, and the work wasn't hard at

all. The best part of the job was that it enabled me to go to school in

the days and work full time at night. The thing that makes me feel good

is that I landed this job all by myself without help from my father or

anyone else.

Step 5. Ordering Your Paragraphs

In addition to planning topic sentences, you must also arrange the elements of your paragraphs in some kind of order as you set them down. Depending upon your purpose and the kinds of materials you are using, you will probably order most of your paragraphs in one of the following ways:

1. Time order—details arranged chronologically (first to last)
2. Space order—details arranged by spatial relationship (left to right, right to left, near to far, far to near, low to high, high to low)
3. Climactic (or emphatic) order—details arranged by importance (least important to most important)
4. Order of complexity—details arranged by difficulty (least difficult to most difficult)
5. Cause to effect order—details arranged by causal relationship (A causes B)

TIME ORDER

Material for three kinds of paragraphs falls naturally into time order with little effort by the writer. Historical discussions and anecdotes (brief stories) nearly always follow time order—that is, they relate the details of an episode according to what happened first. The time method is also used for a set of instructions explaining a process: how to repair a bicycle tire, how to roast a duck, how to flock a Christmas tree, how to clean a revolver. The steps must be explained in the order that they take place, or the reader will be hopelessly confused.

Because time order is usually simple and convenient to follow, however, students often try to adapt it to material for which it is not suited. Many freshman English teachers who have assigned a theme entitled "Why I Want to Go to College" have been forced to wade through a stack of papers which begin "Last year as a high school senior . . ." or even "When I was in the seventh grade . . ." And even more often a student who wants to write about a particularly exciting afternoon hunt will bore the reader with frequent and unnecessary chronological details: "We got up at 5:30 in the morning . . ."

Before you decide to use time order you should therefore consider two questions: (1) Is chronology important to the material, or are you principally concerned with ideas? (2) What elements of chronology are important to your central purpose and which ones are unnecessary and dull?

If you are writing exposition, *you will probably not want to use time order for the entire paper.* Within the theme two or three individual paragraphs may be structured by the time method, but the paragraph containing the thesis—and very likely another paragraph or two—will probably be organized in some other way. For illustration turn again to the two student themes in Step 2. On first reading they both appear to be entirely narrative (time order) papers. But on closer examination you see that in "Listening at Last" only the second half of paragraph 2 and most of paragraph 3 are structured by time order. In "Gregory" most of paragraph 2 and the second half of paragraph 3 are structured by time order.

Time Order—Anecdote

A brief narrative or story which appears within a larger composition (or speech) is called an *anecdote.*

Expository introduction

Father had a lively vocabulary of four-letter words which he called forth readily. He was especially free with those words when one of his employees failed to show up for work, for anyone who wouldn't charge out of bed with a temperature of 104° to be at his desk

Time-order-anecdote

by 8:55 was nothing but a malingerer. One morning while Father was sprinting to work at his usual pace, he slipped on some ice a few doors from his office and had to be carted off by ambulance for a two-month stay in the hospital. Mother was out of town at the time of his fall, and she was unable to get to the hospital to see him until the next day. As she left the elevator and started down the corridor, she heard his voice booming Anglo-Saxon curses at someone and feared he was blasting some poor nurse's aid or orderly for not keeping the ice off all the sidewalks in town. But as she came to his room, she could see him holding up a small hand mirror and thundering profane suggestions about where his reflection should go.

Although this paragraph is entertaining, it is also highly informative and reveals many things about the writer's father: he swears readily; he is impatient with illness; he yells at his employees; he believes in punctuality; he is physically vigorous; he has a resonant voice; he blames innocent people; and most important, he gets angry with himself. Anecdotes which merely entertain are useful to the public speaker who must keep his listeners' minds from wandering, but they serve no purpose in most written composition. In writing exposition you are concerned mainly with ideas. You must use only anecdotes which illustrate some point you are trying to make, and you must keep those anecdotes brief so they will not detract from your major purpose.

Time Order—Process

A set of instructions explaining how to do something is called a process.

Topic sentence

You can make a beautiful flower arrangement with only three blossoms. Select the palest and smallest blossom, but make sure it has a long, straight

Instructions

stem. If necessary, remove the outer petals to make the blossom smaller. Cut the tip of the stem diagonally with a knife so the flower can drink plenty of water, and insert the stem slightly off center in your frog. Next cut the stem of the largest and darkest blossom so that the flower will barely show above the rim of the bowl. Insert the stem in the frog so the blossom tips slightly outward. Then cut the stem of the middle-sized blossom so that it is about a third as tall as the highest one. Insert the stem of this blossom between the other two and fill up the empty spaces with pussy willow or greenery.

A book explaining the history and theory of flower arranging might well contain instructions for many simple arrangements like the one above. In the same way, a recipe book will contain scores of process paragraphs explaining how to mix the ingredients of various recipes.

Pumpkin Chiffon Pie

3 eggs, separated
1 cup sugar
1 cup canned pumpkin
½ cup milk
1 tablespoon unflavored gelatin
¼ cup water
½ teaspoon salt
½ teaspoon ginger
½ teaspoon nutmeg
½ teaspoon cinnamon
pinch cloves

Combine egg yolks, one-half cup sugar, pumpkin, milk, and spices in double boiler and cook until thick. Add gelatin soaked in water. Cool until partially set; then add egg whites stiffly beaten with remaining sugar. Spoon gently into crumb or pastry shell.

These instructions were obviously written for an experienced cook who could recognize the violations of time order within them. A beginner, on the other hand, could very easily have a baking failure as a result of following the steps in the order that they are set down. The instructions do not state explicitly that the gelatin should be put to soak in the water first, and an inexperienced cook might not let the gelatin soak long enough to dissolve properly. More important, the instructions tell the cook to beat the egg yolks first. An experienced cook knows that either he must beat the egg whites first or else he must wash the egg beater after he beats the yolks. But a beginner would probably follow the directions as outlined here and then wonder why the pie was not as light and airy as it should be.

Unfortunately, the writers of process paragraphs too often assume that their readers know as much about the subjects as they do. Obviously, it is always better to give too many instructions than too few and to put them carefully in the exact order.

SPACE ORDER

The physical appearance of something—a pretty girl, a thoroughbred horse, a formal garden, a city skyscraper—usually calls for the organization of details into some kind of spatial relationship. For instance, you might describe the skyscraper by starting at the ground and working up to the top. Or you might describe the flowers in the garden as they appear from left to right, right to left, or near to far.

The effectiveness of space organization is dependent, as is all good writing, upon the quality of the details—their accuracy, their freshness, their concreteness. But sometimes students will present good details in such a jumbled fashion that the reader cannot visualize what is being talked about. Careful attention to space order adds clarity and interest to most physical description.

Topic sentence

First set of details

As we left the square and walked down the chipped and uneven cobblestone path to the river, the street took on a new appearance entirely. The first block was a cluster of tiny shops which looked and smelled of an antique era— a corner spa, a second-hand furniture store, a yarn shop where old women hobbled to gossip away long afternoons, a barber shop with a broken and

Second set of details

Third set of details

Fourth set of details

Fifth set of details

faded pole in front. Next came the houses, block after block of them, all needing paint, and all bordered with scrawny hedges of lilac and honey-suckle. On our left we passed an old red brick church with a low wrought-iron fence to keep out the dogs and a blue neon sign with reminded us "Jesus Saves." After that the houses seemed newer and sturdier, and interspersed among them were apartment houses with stone facades or bright-colored doors. Nearly to the river on the right was the shiny big supermarket where married students came on special days to buy their wives 99-cent orchids.

The details in this paragraph are totally dependent upon their space order, for the topic sentence would have no meaning at all if the information were arranged any other way. Not all scenes lend themselves to such obvious treatment, however, nor can you handle all spatial relationships in terms of a leisurely walk.

Expository introduction

Details

Having come from the bright sun-light outdoors, I couldn't make out much of the dim room at first. There was a small glare to my right which I finally recognized as a cracked mirror hanging on the wall and reflecting a wedge of sunlight from a hole in the curtain on the window opposite. My eyes caught another light object near the mirror, and I could tell it was some white cloth—yes, the fisherman's under-wear that he had drooped over a clothesline to dry. By then I could see fairly well, and my eyes followed around the room to my left—a gas stove on spindly legs, a wooden rocker, and a metal bed covered with a patchwork quilt.

Here the writer has observed the logical procedure of describing the eye-catching objects first and then moving around the room in space order. Even in well-lighted rooms there will usually be one object most likely to capture the attention of someone who enters. But the immediate description of such an object need not prevent the spatial organization of other details.

Likewise, it is usually the face or head of a human being which first captures the attention of someone else.

Topic sentence

As usual Madeline was overdressed. Her hair stuck out from her head in a graying frizz, and black horn-rimmed glasses encircled her eyes. From her ears hung red pendant earrings which

Details

bobbed as she talked, and about her thick neck was a matching strand of red baubles. Her white blouse was ruffled at the elbows, and her red dirndl skirt was embroidered with black and white flowers. On her feet were black

Restatement of
topic idea

patent high-heeled sandals. Every inch of her seemed to scream for attention.

This, then, is a common way to describe a person: to begin with the head and to work down to the ground. If Madeline had been less gaudily dressed, however, and one part of her costume had been more noticeable than the rest, the logical procedure might have been to turn to that part of her outfit first and then shift to space order.

Animals other than human beings may be described by space order.

Topic sentence

However ugly he may be by your standards, the armadillo is properly designed for the kind of life he leads. From his long narrow snout he sticks out an even longer tongue to sweep up

Details

all the spiders, worms, and insects in his path—a menu he finds both delicious and effortless. He probably wouldn't eat steak and corn-on-the-cob even if he could, but of course he can't since he has no front teeth with which to bite them. Farther up his head from his nearly toothless mouth are two small eyes and two rounded ears which look a bit like a teddy bear's although not nearly so cuddly. In fact, he isn't cuddly at all. His back is a hard shell of closely-fitted plates jointed in the middle to permit him to curl into a hard ball in case of danger. From his shell projects a long, pointed tail, the end of which measures about two feet from the tip of his snout on the other end.

The spatial details here make a complete cycle. The paragraph starts at one end of the animal, works slowly to the other end, and then returns to the starting point.

Space order, then, offers many variations of arrangement but depends upon careful observation of details.

Climactic (or Emphatic) Order

Although time order and space order are the two most obvious methods of arranging paragraphs, you will find climactic order to be much more versatile and effective in expository composition. Used not only within paragraphs but within sentences (see p. 155) and within entire compositions, the method is not difficult to master and may indeed be the most valuable technique of writing that you will ever learn. It simply means that you take advantage of the fact that the reader remembers best what he reads last and therefore you build up to a climax by piling more important details upon weaker ones.

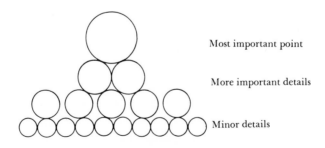

Climactic (Emphatic) Order

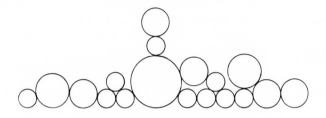

Unemphatic Order

ORDER OF COMPLEXITY

In explaining difficult or complicated material to your reader, you will probably begin with easy or familiar examples and work up to your main point. This method resembles climactic order but is used for somewhat different purposes.

CAUSE TO EFFECT ORDER

Explanatory or argumentative paragraphs will often trace the relationship between a cause and its effect. Cause to effect order is of course similar to time order because a sequence of events is involved in both. For examples of cause to effect paragraphs, see p. 93.

Exercises

A. Theme Assignment

Using one of the informal outlines below, write a theme of 300-500 words containing a time-order anecdote and a time-order process paragraph. Pay attention to Good Introductions on p. 26, and make certain that all paragraphs develop their topic sentences and support the overall thesis. Take particular care to join paragraphs with adequate transitions so that the paragraphs function as parts of the whole theme rather than as independent units. Compose your own title.

1st paragraph:	Some people do not understand drag racing (or some other hobby) because _____. (Thesis)
2nd paragraph:	A story which illustrates misconceptions about drag racing. (Anecdote developed by time order)
3rd paragraph:	Procedures in drag racing. (Process paragraph developed by time order)
4th paragraph:	Benefits or values in drag racing. (Paragraph developed by climactic order)
5th paragraph:	Steps which might be taken to change public opinion about drag racing. (Conclusion developed by climactic order)

1st paragraph:	Young people should realize that there are right and wrong ways to apply for a job. (Thesis)
2nd paragraph:	Wrong way to apply for a job. (Anecdote developed by time order)
3rd paragraph:	Right way to apply for a job. (Process paragraph developed by time order)
4th paragraph:	Benefits derived from the correct approach in job hunting. (Conclusion developed by climactic order)

or

A quotation which supports the thesis. (Conclusion)

1st paragraph:	Some women spend more money in beauty shops than they need to. (Thesis)
2nd paragraph:	Beauty operators often create monsters. (Anecdote developed by time order)
3rd paragraph:	Procedures for styling hair at home. (Process paragraph developed by time order)
4th paragraph:	Advantages of setting one's hair at home. (Conclusion developed by climactic order)

B. Optional Theme Assignment

Using one of the informal outlines below, write a theme of 300-500 words containing two descriptive paragraphs developed by space order. Pay attention to Good Introductions on p. 26, and make certain that all paragraphs develop their topic sentences and support the overall thesis. Take particular care to join paragraphs with adequate transitions so that the paragraphs function as parts of the whole theme rather than as independent units. Compose your own title.

1st paragraph: _____'s appearance attracts attention. (Thesis)

2nd paragraph: What _____ looks like. (Descriptive paragraph developed by space order)

3rd paragraph: How _____ dresses. (Descriptive paragraph developed by space order)

4th paragraph: Why I think _____'s appearance is unique. (Conclusion developed by climactic order)

or

An anecdote about _____'s appearance. (Conclusion)

1st paragraph: I find _____ kind of architecture interesting. (Thesis)

2nd paragraph: A walk through a fascinating part of town. (Descriptive paragraph developed by space order)

3rd paragraph: An unusual house or building. (Descriptive paragraph developed by space order)

4th paragraph: Reasons why _____ architecture appeals to me. (Conclusion developed by climactic order)

Step 6. Using Detail and Illustration

Probably the most common fault in all student exposition is the failure to provide adequate proof for the topic sentence of each paragraph. The topic sentence is merely the skeleton of a paragraph, and that skeleton needs flesh and muscle (substance) before it can do its work within a composition.

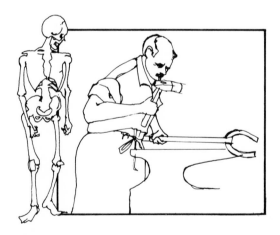

Assigned to write a paragraph on Communism, for example, a student will often string together a series of generalizations (topic sentences) or keep repeating the same generalization over and over in a pattern something like the following:

Communism is the most evil force in the world today. Based upon lies and deceit, Communism is a threat to all mankind. Our God-given freedom is likely to be taken away at any moment by wicked and designing men, but the people of the western world don't seem to care. They sit back in mute apathy waiting for "George" to solve their problems. But there isn't any "George." Every man must recognize the danger of Communism for himself. Every person in America should study what Communism is all about so he can help protect the Constitution from the evil forces of Socialism at home and abroad.

Surely you recognize this paragraph as an example of very poor writing, perhaps without knowing exactly why. But closer inspection reveals that it is empty and meaningless because none of the general statements have been explained, proved, or illustrated in any way. (That the statements may be true is beside the point.) They are merely reworded. Breaking the paragraph into its elements reveals the following structure:

Communism is the most evil force in the world today.	1st general statement
Based upon lies and deceit . . .	re-phrasing of 1st general statement
. . . Communism is a threat to all mankind.	2nd general statement
Our God-given freedom is likely to be taken away at any moment . . .	re-phrasing of 2nd general statement
. . . by wicked and designing men . . .	re-phrasing of 1st general statement
. . . but the people of the western world don't seem to care.	3rd general statement
They sit back in mute apathy waiting for "George" to solve their problems.	re-phrasing of 3rd general statement
But there isn't any "George."	4th general statement
Every man must recognize the danger of Communism for himself.	re-phrasing of 4th general statement

Every person in America should study what Communism is all about so he can help protect the Constitution from the evil forces of Socialism at home and abroad.

re-phrasing of 1st, 2nd, and 4th general statements.

At least four points emerge from our examination of this paragraph:

1. Every generalization should be proved (re-phrasing a generalization does not prove it).

2. Important generalizations should be used as the topic sentences for their own paragraphs, not buried in other paragraphs.

3. Obvious or trivial general statements are insulting to the reader's intelligence and should be discarded (*e.g.,* "But there isn't any 'George.' ").

4. The "paragraph" on Communism above is not a paragraph at all but a series of topic sentences calling for three or four paragraphs.

Properly, the student should have limited his paragraph to the first topic sentence—*Communism is the most evil force in the world today.* Paying attention to the controlling idea, *evil force,* he could then establish his point either by use of (a) detail or (b) illustration.

a. To establish the topic sentence by use of *detail* the writer might turn to recent speeches by leaders in Russia, China, or Cuba to see what the current policy is toward armaments, coexistence, freedom of worship, private ownership, uncensored news, family life, and the like. Or he might turn to the official news releases from these countries to learn about wages and hours, cost of living, medical services, and government controls. Possibly he could read articles by qualified American economists, political scientists, sociologists, and religious leaders. But a paragraph developed by detail must contain specific information and facts which make up a whole picture. (The use of judgments or opinions in paragraph development will be discussed in Step 9.)

b. To establish the same topic sentence by use of *illustration* the writer might give one example or several to show how a Communist minority has taken over such a government as Hungary. Or he might show how particular citizens in Communist countries have been imprisoned, tortured, or in some other way deprived of their civil liberties. An illustration, then, is a narrative example. One such example may occupy the entire paragraph (see the anecdote in Step 5), or the topic sentence may be supported by a series of brief examples within one paragraph.

The following sample paragraphs will point up the difference between detail and illustration.

Detail

To obtain a job as a pilot for most of the commercial airlines an applicant must meet the following requirements: (1) high school diploma plus two years of college or equivalent experience; (2) height between 5 feet 7 inches and 6 feet 4 inches with weight in proportion; (3) 20/20 vision; (4) age between 20 and 30; and (5) a minimum of 400 flying hours. In addition the applicant must pass the airline's written examination as well as physical examinations given by both the airline and the Federal Aviation Agency.

In the foregoing paragraph the requirements for commercial airlines pilots have been broken down into specific details, most of which are numbered for our convenience. The details in the next paragraph, however, are not so clearly labeled:

Aluminum is a pale silver metal which is manufactured from bauxite ore. Unusually light, aluminum can be stretched into almost any shape, and an object made from it weighs about one-third as much as the same object made from iron or steel. When alloyed with other metals, aluminum becomes strong enough for the construction of buildings or airplane wings. Aluminum can also be stretched into thin gum wrappers or fine wire. Because of its conductivity and light weight, aluminum wire is frequently used to carry electric current. It is also rust-proof, non-magnetic, and nonsparking. It seldom needs to be painted or otherwise protected.

Both paragraphs—on requirements for airlines pilots and qualities of aluminum—are developed by a series of single parts which make up a larger picture. Details are therefore basic parts or facts that make up a whole.

Illustration

Topic sentence	The Puritans of early America employed various tests to decide whether or not accused persons were witches. One such test was to submit the accused to embarrassing physical examinations to look for strange teats or warts on the body. Another test was to ask the suspect to recite the Lord's Prayer, for a witch would be unable to speak the holy words in the correct order. More painful tests included pricking the suspect with pins, thrusting her hands into boiling water, or throwing her into a large body of water. If she reacted to pain or was drowned, she was innocent.
1st illustration	
2nd illustration	
3rd illustration	
4th illustration	
5th illustration	

This paragraph illustrates the controlling idea, *tests to decide whether persons were witches,* with five examples of what the Puritans *did.* In other words, each of these examples is a very brief story.

Again the principle of illustration can be seen in the following paragraph:

Topic sentence	The guests who go to Viewmont Inn are the laziest vacationers in the world. While the tennis court collects dust and the swimming pool sparkles silently in the sun, the patrons gather on the sun deck to read, chat, or engage in a cautious game of dominoes. Even eating is too great an effort for most guests, who rise about ten, eat a leisurely brunch at eleven, and sometimes forget to return to the dining room for supper until late evening. The attitude at Viewmont is that vacationing means resting—and only resting. Anyone who should bring fishing equipment to the Inn to use at one of the nearby streams would surely be whispered about by the other guests.
1st illustration	
2nd illustration	
Restatement of topic idea	
3rd illustration	

Each of the illustrations in this paragraph tells what the vacationers do and is a brief narrative example to prove that Viewmont guests are lazy.

Because detail and illustration are closely related, students sometimes have difficulty understanding the difference between them. It is helpful to remember, however, that although illustration (example) usually incorporates detail (basic facts), detail cannot incorporate illustration. But you need not worry if you cannot readily distinguish between the two. What is important is that both kinds of writing are specific and informative and lend substance and interest to the general ideas expressed in the topic sentences.

Exercises

A. Theme Assignment

Using one of the informal outlines below, write a theme of 400-500 words containing paragraphs developed by detail and illustration. Pay attention to Good Introductions on p. 26, and make certain that all paragraphs develop their topic sentences and support the overall thesis. Take particular care to join paragraphs with adequate transitions so that the paragraphs function as parts of the whole theme rather than as independent units. Compose your own title.

1st paragraph: The American highway is more dangerous than it should be. (Thesis)
2nd paragraph: Traffic accidents need not happen. (Paragraph developed by illustration)
3rd paragraph: Cars could be made safer. (Paragraph developed by detail)
4th paragraph: Quotation in support of the thesis. (Conclusion)

1st paragraph: College has become highly competitive. (Thesis)
2nd paragraph: Entrance requirements are becoming more difficult. (Paragraph developed by detail)
3rd paragraph: Classes are getting larger. (Paragraph developed by illustration)
4th paragraph: Frustrations are mounting. (Concluding anecdote)

1st paragraph: Magazine advertisements are uneven in quality. (Thesis)

2nd paragraph:	Examples of poor advertisements. (Paragraph developed by illustration)
3rd paragraph:	Elements of one poor advertisement. (Paragraph developed by detail)
4th paragraph:	Examples of good advertisements. (Paragraph developed by illustration)
5th paragraph:	Elements of one good advertisement. (Paragraph developed by detail)

B. Optional Theme Assignment

Using one of the topics below, expand your own thesis statement and informal outline into a theme of 400-500 words. Underline the thesis in your first paragraph, and indicate in the margin which paragraphs are developed by detail and which by illustration. Compose your own title.

Chaperones
Getting along with roommates
Dating by computer
Exchange students
A topic related to another college course you are currently taking

Step 7. Using Comparison/Contrast

When you *compare* two or more things, you point out their similarities. When you contrast two or more things, you point out their differences. Nearly always when you discuss things side by side, however, you will find it necessary both to compare and to contrast.

The technique of comparison and contrast is useful in exposition because

1. it forces you to consider your material carefully.

2. it forces you to use specific details and examples.

3. it encourages you to arrange your material logically.

4. it contributes to the reader's understanding.

Because this expository technique demands such careful attention by the writer, college teachers will frequently compose essay tests in which the student is obliged to compare and contrast two such things as militarism under Kaiser Wilhelm II and Adolph Hitler, eye structures of the bee and the ant, or poems by Wordsworth and Shelley.

You may extend comparison and contrast throughout an entire composition or limit it to a single paragraph. A typical example follows:

The principal difference between the American and the Japanese woman is that although neither one knows how to converse, the Japanese woman doesn't even try to. Not knowing how to converse doesn't keep the American woman from talking, of course. She is always talking—about diets, bowling scores, PTA meetings, Cub Scout programs, beauty operators, color schemes, garden pests, brand names, and the like. But with the possible exception of a limited number of issues concerned with the problems of rearing her children, the American woman does not know how to discuss an *idea*. The Japanese woman, on the other hand, knows that her thoughts aren't worth expressing, so she doesn't even try. Instead, she has developed the art of asking those questions which encourage men to talk and then of sitting in rapt attention while her husband or lover expounds.

This paragraph compares by saying that the American and Japanese woman are alike because neither can converse. It contrasts by saying that the American and Japanese woman are different because the American woman tries to converse even when she doesn't know how. The student has placed all of the information about the American woman at the beginning and all of the information about the Japanese woman at the end. Such a method may be successful within a paragraph, but an entire composition which compares and contrasts should be divided less sharply. You will do better to alternate your objects of discussion from one paragraph to another or to insert an occasional paragraph in which the two things are discussed detail by detail. The following paragraph demonstrates the latter method.

> Like Lincoln, William McGuffey had been born to poor parents—a father with little ambition other than to hunt, a mother who taught her children the scriptures and dreamed of their future success. Like Lincoln, he was tall, raw-boned, strong, and homely. Like Lincoln, he was obedient, responsible, and hardworking. Like Lincoln, he thirsted for knowledge and was known to walk miles to borrow any kind of book. Like Lincoln, he was to influence the pattern of 19th-century American thought. But unlike Lincoln, he was not to be remembered and loved as a person long after his death.
> Comparing McGuffey and Lincoln detail by detail, this para-

graph illustrates also how you can use parallel sentence structure to bind the elements of comparison/contrast material together. (For more information on the use of parallelism as a transitional device, see p. 53.)

ANALOGY

A comparison between two things which are basically different but which have similar qualities is called an analogy:

> Polishing a speech for a public performance is something like altering a dress to be worn to a party. Like the dress, the speech should be examined carefully to make certain that it is suitable

to the occasion for which it will be used. It should next be prac-
ticed in the same way that the dress should be modeled before a
mirror. Necessary tucks and expansions will then become more
apparent, as will other alterations to make the speech interesting and attractive. Finally the speaker, like the dressmaker,
should remember the importance of overall length.

The foregoing paragraph might be useful in a book on public speaking prepared for adult women of limited education. Likewise a high
school science teacher might explain nuclear fission to his students
in terms of a chain reaction started by ping pong balls bumping into
each other. In other words, an analogy attempts to explain something that is unfamiliar by comparing it to something which is readily understood.

Useful as it can be when properly employed, the analogy has
limitations, too. Because the two things being compared will always
be dissimilar in some major respect, no absolute conclusion can ever
be drawn from an analogy. Obvious as this statement may sound, experienced writers as well as beginners often yield to the temptation
to argue from an analogy.

In 1928, for instance, long before Great Britain nationalized
many of its industries, the British scientist J. B. S. Haldane argued
that there was a correct size and shape for every living animal and
that for any creature to change size would also require a change of
form. Having proved his thesis with many examples from the animal
kingdom, he then went on to argue that there must also be a right
size for "every human institution." Socialism, he concluded, might
work in a small country but not in the entire British Empire or the
United States.

Whether or not socialism could work in the entire British Empire or the United States is still being debated by political scientists
and economists and is not really of concern here. What does matter
is that Haldane was guilty of a logical error by arguing from an
analogy. The foolishness of his statement can perhaps be more readily seen if the argument is turned around:

> The United States government is the best government in the
> world. Therefore all spiders should elect a president and two
> houses of Congress to make and carry out laws.

Remember, therefore, that analogies are useful for explanation
but should never be used for persuasion.

Exercises

A. Theme Assignment

Using one of the informal outlines below, write a theme of 400-500 words containing paragraphs developed by comparison and/or contrast. Pay attention to Good Introductions on p. 26; and make certain that all paragraphs develop their topic sentences and support the overall thesis. Take particular care to join paragraphs with adequate transitions. Compose your own title.

1st paragraph: Teenagers haven't really changed since Mother's and Dad's day. (Thesis)

2nd paragraph: Differences in financial or educational opportunities. (Paragraph developed by contrast)

3rd paragraph: Similarities in dress. (Paragraph developed by comparison)

4th paragraph: Similarities in musical taste. (Paragraph developed by comparison)

5th paragraph: Similarities in attitudes. (Paragraph developed by comparison)

1st paragraph: _____ is an interesting place to visit, but I would prefer to live in _____. (Thesis)

2nd paragraph: Scenic beauty in _____ and _____ _____. (Paragraph developed by comparison and contrast)

3rd paragraph: Recreation in _____ and _____. (Paragraph developed by comparison and contrast)

4th paragraph: Professional opportunities in _____ and _____. (Paragraph developed by comparison and contrast)

5th paragraph: People in _____ and _____. (Paragraph developed by comparison and contrast)

B. Optional Theme Assignment

Using one of the entries below, expand your own thesis statement and informal outline into a 500-word theme of comparison and contrast. Pay attention to Good Introductions on p. 26, and underline the thesis in your first paragraph. Be careful to see that the thesis limits the material to a narrow aspect of the topic which can be developed in 500 words.

Two famous Americans

Education in America and some other country (from firsthand experience)

Automobiles then and now (choose a definite time; do not generalize)

Beauty aids then and now (choose a definite time; do not generalize)

Beauty pageants and dog shows

Two kinds of rebels

Two styles of painting

Two kinds of music

Two American magazines

Step 8. Using Analysis and Definition

ANALYSIS

Coming from the Greek word for "a breaking up," *analysis* means to divide something into parts which can be studied separately. In writing, the method of analysis is particularly useful for material which is complex or unfamiliar to the reader:

> A Russian child who has completed the eight-year common school may be permitted to enroll in one of several upper secondary schools: three-year schools, technicums and special schools, or labor schools. The three-year schools emphasize science, mathematics, and other academic subjects which prepare students for university work. Not all graduates of these schools go on to college, of course, and in recent years more emphasis has been placed on technical and vocational training. The technicums provide semi-professional training for laboratory technicians, nurses, and some kinds of engineers. Students remain at technicum for from three to five years. Labor schools operate in conjunction with factories and farms, providing practical experience for their students. Graduates must remain in the type of work for which they have been trained for a minimum of four years.

In addition, material which introduces terms which are unfamiliar to the reader is often best handled by analysis:

> The two main types of rowing races are (1) sculling and (2) sweep-oar rowing. In sculling, both the boat and the oars are

called sculls. Each oarsman, or sculler, uses two oars, and the scull craft will usually seat from one to four men although 8-man sculls are sometimes used. In sweep-oar rowing, each man uses only one oar, which is much longer than a sculling oar. These boats will seat two, four, six, or eight men and often an additional coxswain. The coxswain steers the rudder and directs the timing of the oar strokes.

Even simple material, however, can often be broken into two or more parts:

American mothers too commonly fall into one of three classes: (1) the watch-out-or-you'll-break-yourself type, (2) the watch-out-or-you'll-break-something-else type, and the (3) go-away-and-stop-bothering-me type. The first type hovers constantly over her little one to make certain that no big bad virus overpowers him or that no bigger child interferes with his rights. She sterilizes his bottles until he is nine months old, takes his temperature regularly, and stands guard over his sand box like a fierce giant. The second type of mother is ever alert to her child's dependence upon her, for she knows he cannot do anything right. She re-combs his hair, re-ties his shoe-laces, and re-washes the dishes he had so carefully dried and put away. The third type of mother likes to think that she is teaching her child independence by staying out of his life, but actually she is too lazy and too selfish to teach him anything except that he is a nuisance.

Analysis is often useful in introducing a subject. For instance, a paper devoted to one recommended method for refinishing a chair might briefly mention one or two other ways of refinishing furniture. But you should limit the space you devote to nonessentials and be wary of talking at length about things that you really did not intend to talk about at all.

One final suggestion: Before submitting to the temptation of letting all elements of analysis follow a numbering system, turn again to the alternative proposal on p. 33.

DEFINITION

People sometimes assume that all words have exact meanings and that any question of definition can be easily settled by consulting a dictionary. But although abstract words such as *love, faith, family, honor, pride* are understood in a general way by nearly everyone, no dictionary can account for the special meanings they carry on different occasions. *Family,* for instance, means one thing the day of a happy boat trip with your brothers and sisters and quite another the day of a quarrel with your father over the use of the car. Obviously, the limited dictionary definition which says a family consists of "parents and children whether living together or not" is not very useful in either situation.

atheist

Jewish rabbi

Buddhist priest

Salem housewife

Methodist missionary

Navaho Indian

Russian Communist

Even more troublesome are those words which carry widely different meanings for persons of different backgrounds and prejudices. For example, how can a dictionary define a word like *religion* in terms that would be equally acceptable to a Methodist missionary, a Jewish rabbi, a Navaho Indian, a Russian Communist, an atheist who bitterly opposes prayer in the public schools, a Salem housewife about to be hanged for witchcraft, or a Buddhist priest contemplating suicide in Vietnam?

It is therefore often necessary for you to explain to your reader exactly what you mean by a particular word. Such a definition will probably occupy at least a paragraph and may extend to a long theme or even an entire book. Because of its length and treatment, this kind of explanation is usually called an *extended definition* or an *amplified definition.* The most common uses for extended definitions are (1) to explain a difficult term with which the reader may not be familiar, or (2) to explain terms that different people may interpret in different ways.

Before developing your own definition, you may find it helpful to refer to the dictionary in order to familiarize yourself with points which had not occurred to you. But in no way are you limited to what you read there. In fact, you may even contradict the dictionary as long as your own definition is clear and reasonable.

Of the five most common ways to develop an extended definition, three depend upon methods already discussed in this book:

1. Illustration (Step 6)
2. Comparison and contrast (Step 7)
3. Analysis (above)
4. History or development
5. Exclusion

Definition by Illustration (Example)

You may define a word by showing how its concept *operates,* as in the definition of *prejudice* below:

Topic sentence	Prejudices, or pre-judgments, are made before any real evidence has been examined and therefore operate both between and within social and eco-
1st example	nomic groups. Negroes and whites are
2nd example	prejudiced against each other, but both are prejudiced against members of their own races who marry outsiders.
3rd example	College graduates and non-college graduates eye each other with suspi-

4th example	cion, but Harvard men look with disdain upon graduates from NYU. In-
5th example	door hobbyists and outdoor sportsmen do not even try to understand each
6th example	other's interests, but a fly-rod purist views a bait fisherman with pure loath-ing.

Definition by Comparison and Contrast

A word may be defined by pairing it with another word closely related to it—such as *house* and *home, compromise* and *cooperation, knowledge* and *wisdom, grooming* and *taste,* or *recipe* and *direction* —to point up the differences and similarities in meaning:

Similarity	Recipes and directions are both con-
Difference	cerned with desired ends, but a direc-tion merely points to the end whereas a recipe provides the formula or method for achieving it. The difference can be illustrated from my own life.
Illustration	When I was a child, my father was al-ways telling me what he expected of me in life: make friends, win a letter in football, graduate from college, and be-come a success in the business world. But it was not until after I had made many mistakes and wondered if I could ever possibly please him that I realized he had only set up the goals, or direc-tions. Never once had he bothered to prescribe a method, or recipe.

Definition by Analysis

You may define a word by placing it in a general class and then explaining how it differs from other members of the same class:

The term	*Its general class*	*How it is different*
A piano	is a musical instrument	in which hammers oper-ated from a keyboard strike upon metal strings
A mackerel	is a fish of the North Atlantic	with wavy cross markings on the back and stream-lined shape for swim-ming.

| A Nisei | is a person of Japanese descent | who was born in the U.S.A. and is loyal to it. |
| An honor system | is a scheme of management for schools and other institutions | whereby obedience to rules is sought by granting personal responsibility rather than imposing guards, restrictions, and physical force. |

This kind of definition by analysis is the method most often used by dictionaries but can also be extended to the length of a paragraph or more:

| The term and its general class | The honor system is a scheme of management which has been conducted successfully at some American universities for many |
| How it is different | years. At institutions operating under the system, students will take examinations with no proctors in the room and will even be permitted to leave the classroom to get a drink of water or talk on the telephone. Instead of being watched, they may sign pledges indicating that they neither gave nor received unpermitted aid during the examination. The honor system also extends to personal belongings, and seldom do institutions operating under it receive complaints of theft or vandalism. One coed at a west coast university left her purse containing more than fifty dollars in plain sight on the lawn and three days later found it in the exact spot where she had mislaid it. |

Definition by History

You may define a word by showing the changes in meaning that it has taken on over a long period of time:

	An advertisement was once a modest
Earliest advertisement	thing: an announcement by the town crier or a hand-written notice of an "offer for sale" posted in the public square. But early in the
In 1800's	1800's the influence of salesmanship became apparent in the public notice. By the time of

In 1860's

the Civil War "advertising agents" were buying space in newspapers and magazines which they then resold to merchants at a commission of about fifteen percent. To help the advertiser, the agent would assist in planning the notice for emphasis and the most

Advertising today

profitable use of advertising space. Today's advertising agents are men and women who receive millions of dollars annually for writing jingles and slogans, preparing cartoons, and generally trying to make the public think that some product is better than it really is.

Definition by Exclusion

You may define a word by showing what it is not, rather than what it is:

1st exclusion

Responsibility is not something which you can acquire from reading books on the sub-

2nd exclusion
3rd exclusion

ject. It is not something you learn about from being lectured to. You cannot develop responsibility by talking about it with other

4th exclusion

people, wise though they may be. You cannot even develop it by watching responsible people in action.

Exercises

A. Theme Assignment

Using one of the informal outlines below, write a theme of 400-500 words containing a paragraph developed by analysis. Pay attention to Good Introductions on p. 26, and make certain that all paragraphs develop their topic sentences and support the overall thesis. Take particular care to join paragraphs with adequate transitions. Compose your own title.

1st paragraph: Even good friends will trap you into disastrous blind dates. (Thesis)

2nd paragraph:	Blind dates fall roughly into 2 (or 3) classes. (Paragraph developed by analysis)
3rd paragraph: 4th paragraph: 5th paragraph:	Illustrations of terrible blind dates. (Paragraphs developed by anecdote)

1st paragraph:	American television is (is not) catering to the thoughtful American. (Thesis)
2nd paragraph:	General types of television shows. (Paragraph developed by analysis)
3rd paragraph: 4th paragraph:	Examples of good (poor) television shows. (Paragraphs developed by illustration)
5th paragraph:	Benefits derived from watching television. (Conclusion)

or

Suggestions for better programing. (Conclusion)

B. Theme Assignment

Using one of the informal outlines below, write a theme of 400-500 words containing a definition. Pay attention to Good Introductions on p. 26; and make certain that all paragraphs develop their topic sentences and support the overall thesis. Take particular care to join paragraphs with adequate transitions. Compose your own title.

1st paragraph:	Young people today cannot communicate with their parents. (Thesis)
2nd paragraph:	Communication means _____. (Paragraph developed by definition)
3rd paragraph: 4th paragraph:	Examples of bad communication. (Paragraphs developed by illustration)
5th paragraph:	Results of poor communication. (Conclusion)

or

Communication can be strengthened by _____ _____. (Conclusion)

1st paragraph:	Cooking is a lost art. (Thesis)
2nd paragraph:	Cooking is not _____. (Definition developed by exclusion)

3rd paragraph:	How Grandma used to cook. (Paragraph developed by illustration)
4th paragraph:	What meals are like today. (Paragraph developed by anecdote)
5th paragraph:	If the present trend continues, meals are likely to become _____. (Definition developed by history and projection)

1st paragraph:	_____(A)_____ will never replace _____(B)_____. (Thesis)
2nd paragraph:	_____(A)_____ means _____. (Paragraph developed by definition)
3rd paragraph:	_____(B)_____ means _____. (Paragraph developed by definition)
4th paragraph:	Comparative advantages of _____(A)_____ and _____(B)_____. (Conclusion by comparison and contrast)

C. Optional Theme Assignments

Using one of the thesis statements below, prepare an informal outline and a theme of 400-500 words organized by analysis.

A good teacher should demonstrate _____ qualities.
Two-legged wolves are of _____ types.
Cigarette smokers are of _____ types.
Teetotalers are of _____ types.
Gum chewers are of _____ types.
Story tellers are of _____ types.
Spectator sports appeal to _____ types of people.
Interior decorators are of _____ types.
Happiness is dependent upon _____ things.
A worthwhile book should have _____ qualities.
Life in 2000 A.D. will be characterized by _____ things.
A theater critic should look for _____ things.

D. Optional Theme Assignments

Write a theme of 400-500 words in which the entire paper defines one of the terms below. Try to use two or more of the following kinds of extended definition: illustration, comparison and contrast, analysis, history, exclusion.

Sophistication
Hippies
Vanity
Innocence
Faith
Conscience
Status symbols
Creativity
Insecurity
Rebellion
Pacifism
Apathy
Isolation

Step 9. Using Reasons

In writing, as in daily experience, problems must sometimes be solved by reason. Why should the school constitution be changed, why do flood waters still pour into basements of homes in certain areas of the city, why does the poetry of Phyllis McGinley appeal to women—all of these are questions which call for reasons. Reasons, then, are opinions or judgments which are formed within the mind. Reasons should be based upon the best facts available, but they are distinguished from them because (1) facts come from sources outside the mind, and (2) facts are more easily proved.

Problem	Reason	Fact
I am happy because	today is a wonderful day	today is my eighteenth birthday
Milk is a good beverage because	it is healthful	it contains carbohydrates, fats, proteins, calcium, vitamin A, riboflavin, and vitamin D
I plan to take Greek mythology because	it is an easy course	last term Professor Meredith gave 12 A's in a class of 23 students

Most exposition calling for reason will follow one of four general patterns: question to answer, problem to solution, cause to effect, or effect to cause.

REASON—QUESTION TO ANSWER

Why would men choose to become gladiators and risk death in the Roman Colosseum? At first gladiators were slaves or prisoners who were forced to participate in the contests. Often they underwent rigid training, and some became so skilled that they earned great popularity. The most successful ones were not only granted their freedom but even won valuable gifts and the attentions of Roman ladies. Soon very poor freemen entered gladiator contests as a means to wealth and fame; and eventually even Roman aristocrats took part in the competitions on an amateur basis.

The question in this paragraph—why would men choose to become gladiators—is answered by reasons as they came about in the course of history. Other questions might be answered by a series of reasons or by a single reason.

REASON—PROBLEM TO SOLUTION

Man's ability to provide food to sustain life is not increasing at the same rate as his own reproduction. Of course it is hoped that western technology will soon make more of the earth's land mass available for agriculture. But that day may never arrive because as more people crowd the earth, the useful productive areas decrease in size. Population control seems the only answer.

This paragraph begins with a problem—overpopulation—moves to a commonly-argued solution—technology—and concludes with the student's solution—birth control. Persuasive prose always follows the climactic or emphatic order, which means that the argument which the writer considers the most important should appear last.

REASON—CAUSE TO EFFECT

Teenagers are quick to rebel at the authority of the older generation but are afraid to rebel at the authority of their own classmates. Straggly hair in their eyes, toeless sandals, sprayed-on jeans, and revealing dresses are all part of their open defiance of adult standards. But they do not have the same courage in deviating from standards of their own peers. High school girls will even call each other in the morning to check what their friends are wearing to school so that they can dress alike.

This paragraph begins with a cause, stated in general terms: teenage conformity to standards of other teenagers. The paragraph then lists specific effects from that cause.

REASON—EFFECT TO CAUSE

Although they were slower and less dangerous than automobiles of today, the first horseless carriages frightened many people for one reason or another. Passengers feared the unreliable engines and constant breakdowns. Railroad companies feared the competition automobiles posed. Farmers feared the danger to horses and cattle. Taxpayers feared the increased financial burdens for improvement of roads. Probably even the inventors themselves feared that their machines would never achieve wide acceptance.

This paragraph begins with an effect—fear of horseless carriages— and then lists several causes for that fear.

All of the foregoing paragraphs use facts as part of the reasons. In general, reasons will answer the question *why,* and facts will answer the questions *what* and *how.*

Exercises

A. Theme Assignment

Using one of the informal outlines below, write a theme of 500-600 words containing a paragraph developed by reason. Compose your own title.

1st paragraph: Cheating is common at _____ University. (Thesis)

2nd paragraph: Why students cheat. (Paragraph developed by reason)

3rd paragraph: How students cheat. (Paragraph developed by factual illustration)

4th paragraph: Results of cheating at _____ University. (Paragraph developed by anecdote)

5th paragraph: Cheating can be prevented by _____.
                (Conclusion)

1st paragraph: Foreign students are (are not) made to feel at
                home by American students at my university.
                (Thesis)
2nd paragraph: An incident which illustrates the thesis. (Para-
                graph developed by anecdote)
3rd paragraph: Why American students feel the way they do.
                (Paragraph developed by reason)
4th paragraph: Why foreign students react the way they do. (Par-
                agraph developed by reason)
5th paragraph: Proposals for improving relations of American
                and foreign students. (Conclusion)
                            or
                Quotation by a foreign student in support of the
                thesis. (Conclusion)

B. Optional Theme Assignment

Using one of the topics listed below, prepare a thesis statement, an
informal outline, and a theme of 500-600 words containing at least
one paragraph developed by reason.

Racial intolerance in America
Religious intolerance in America
Political intolerance in America
Social intolerance in America
Automation
War in the late 20th century
Draft dodgers
Movie censorship
Book burning
Faculty control of student publications
Academic freedom for professors
A change in the voting age
Urban renewal
Fluoridation

Checklist for Paragraphs

☐ 1. Does each main paragraph begin with a topic sentence or a transition sentence followed by a topic sentence?

☐ 2. Have I focused the topic sentence on one aspect of a problem by means of key words (controlling idea)?

☐ 3. Have I developed the controlling idea fully (with four or more additional concrete sentences)?

☐ 4. If I have used short paragraphs, have I done so consciously— for transition, summary, or emphasis?

☐ 5. Have I arranged my thoughts logically so that each paragraph hangs together?

☐ 6. Have I provided additional transitional devices to insure coherence?

☐ 7. Have I used time order only for material in which chronology is important?

☐ 8. If I have used time order, have I limited myself to those elements which are useful to my central purpose?

☐ 9. Have I used detail and illustration rather than generalization?

☐ 10. Have I made effective use of comparison and contrast? Analysis? Definition? Reasons?

☐ 11. If I have used analogy, have I avoided the pitfall of arguing from an analogy?

PART III

Separating the Flair
From the Flapdoodle

Step 10. How to Sidestep Wordiness and Vagueness

When Mark Twain's Huckleberry Finn said his friend the king was "all tears and flapdoodle," he meant the king was wailing and ranting and putting on a show of foolish emotion over the death of someone he had never met. In other words, he was a phony. Flapdoodle in writing, too, is phony nonsense. It occurs when writers are trying to impress their readers rather than trying to communicate with them.

Two of the most common kinds of flapdoodle in writing are wordiness (taking too many words to say something) and vagueness (talking in fuzzy, roundabout language). But although the two problems are defined separately, they nearly always occur together. A writer who "throws in" unnecessary words usually fails to express a clear idea. And a writer who doesn't begin with a clear idea will "throw in" extra words in an effort to set anything on paper. Thus we can look at the two pitfalls of wordiness and vagueness together.

ADJECTIVES VS. NOUNS

For some reason many students do not even want to escape the temptation of adjectives. They are positively determined that adjectives are the colorful, life-giving words which separate skillful writing from ordinary prose. Adjectives, they argue, limit the meanings of nouns and therefore make composition more descriptive and exact. The more adjectives the better!

But before you are persuaded by the logic that adjectives lead to skillful and concrete writing, perhaps you should consider the tongue-in-cheek advice from another Mark Twain character, Pudd'nhead Wilson:

As to the Adjective: when in doubt, strike it out.

Still not convinced? Well, possibly Twain was thinking of sentences something like these:

Wordy and Vague	Concrete and Concise
The small, furry, long-tailed animal scampered across the floor.	The mouse scampered across the floor.
My parent's paternal parent spanked me.	My grandfather spanked me.
The conductor led the orchestra in the fast-slow-fast alternating music.	The conductor led the orchestra in the symphony.
My heavy blue cotton twill work pants have a hole in the knee.	My jeans have a hole in the knee.
The 14-line, rhyming, iambic pentameter composition was written by Shakespeare.	The sonnet was written by Shakespeare.

Despite how extreme these particular sentences may be, they illustrate the principle of good writing which Twain was probably trying to tell us in his roundabout way: *A mountain of adjectives cannot do the work of one exact noun.* In other words, adjectives can narrow or strengthen the meaning of a noun, but they become indirect, awkward, and even confusing when used in place of the noun itself.

Or to turn the principle around: *A single exact noun can convey a clear idea with few or no adjective modifiers:*

Battering the gates of heaven with *storms* of prayer.
                    Tennyson   *St. Simeon Stylites*

Time the *devourer* of all things.
                    Ovid   Metamorphoses

When once the *itch* of literature comes over a man, nothing
can cure it but the *scratching* of a pen.
                    Samuel Lover   *Handy Andy*

The *trumpet* of his own virtues.
                    Shakespeare   *Much Ado About Nothing*

Men's evil manners live in *brass;* their virtues
We write in *water.*
                    Shakespeare   *King Henry VIII*

These nouns are successful because they are concrete. They can be
seen, touched, heard, smelled, or tasted. But vague and concrete are
relative terms, and the writer must often choose not between the
two but between nouns which are concrete and those which are
more concrete still:

I listened to $\begin{cases} \text{the radio} \\ \text{the news} \\ \text{the 10 o'clock news} \end{cases}$

I prepared $\begin{cases} \text{something to eat} \\ \text{dinner} \\ \text{chili and salad} \end{cases}$

I went $\begin{cases} \text{to town} \\ \text{to see the dentist} \\ \text{to see Dr. Ward} \end{cases}$

Vague Adjectives

Often the writer who is careless in his selection of nouns will try
to make those nouns more exact by modifying them with equally
vague adjectives:

The *beautiful, charming* girl entered the room and viewed the
lovely party decorations.

Professor White has taught me *important political* ideals.

Collies respond well to training because they have *tremendous*
minds.

Jolene is a *nice* girl with many *fine* qualities.

It makes me *unhappy* to see the *un-American* principles portrayed
in the *entertainment* media.

A *successful* person is usually one who is *honest, ambitious,* and *well-educated.*

After a *delicious* dinner we moved to the living room for *delight-ful* conversation.

Trite Adjectives

Another temptation is to place adjectives and nouns in tired, worn-out combinations:

Mary Ann flashed her *sparkling* blue eyes.

I cast my fly into the *crystal-clear* water.

The *fluffy* white clouds moved silently over our heads.

We had a *romantic* adventure through Africa.

His *crooked* smile made my heart beat.

The *stately* mansion was framed by *majestic* trees.

The *bubbling* stream flowed down the mountain.

My *clammy* hands gave away my fear.

Adjectives That Act

This discussion is not intended to send you scurrying for a sturdy red pencil with which to blot out every adjective in sight. Even Mark Twain prefaced his advice by saying "When in doubt . . . ," for adjectives which call forth specific sensory impressions are extremely useful in tightening the meaning of a noun. Particularly helpful in crowding action into sentences are those adjectives which have been formed from vigorous verbs.

She stood pouting, the strands of her long hair *bending* and *kinking* like *frayed* orange yarn.

Tugging, hissing, foaming, the waves coaxed the *gutted* stump out to sea.

She struck the piano with hands *yellowed* and *gnarled* as canary claws.

Such adjectives are formed from the present participle and the past participle forms of the verb. The present participle always ends in *ing* and is determined by saying *I am . . .* before the verb stem. The past participle usually (but not always) ends in *d, ed, t, n,* or *en* and is determined by saying *I have . . .* before the verb stem.

Four Principal Parts of a Verb

Present Today I . . .	Past Yesterday I . . .	Past Participle I have . . .	Present Participle I am . . .
frown	frowned	frowned	frowning
whimper	whimpered	whimpered	whimpering
tiptoe	tiptoed	tiptoed	tiptoeing
shiver	shivered	shivered	shivering
tear	tore	torn	tearing
creep	crept	crept	creeping
nestle	nestled	nestled	nestling
wobble	wobbled	wobbled	wobbling
wail	wailed	wailed	wailing
burn	burned	burned	burning

Any verb in these last two columns may be used as an adjective.

For more information about participles, see p. 150.

ADVERBS VS. VERBS

Twain might even more appropriately have warned us about too many adverbs, for their overuse indicates inattention to the most important word in the sentence—the verb. When you find yourself using a great number of adverbs, you can be certain that your verbs are flabby.

Wordy and Flabby	Concise and Forceful
The chickadee sang tremulously and intermittently from the sumac.	The chickadee twittered from the sumac.
Harshly and shrilly the old woman called to the child in the street.	The old woman screeched at the child in the street.

Grandpa walked unsteadily down the alley.	Grandpa tottered down the alley.
Red-faced and shaking with rage, the sergeant yelled loudly and harshly at the recruit.	Red-faced and shaking with rage, the sergeant flayed the recruit.
The dog drew back fearfully.	The dog flinched.

No other part of speech is worthy of the care in selection that the verb is, for no other part of speech is capable of such fire and ice:

> You should have *banged* the youth into dumbness.
> > Shakespeare   *Twelfth Night*
>
> Then Tomlinson he *gripped* the bars and *yammered,* "Let me in——"
> > Kipling   *Tomlinson*
>
> For we know that the whole creation *groaneth* and *travaileth* in pain until now.
> > Romans 8:22
>
> Johnson: Well, we had a good talk.
> Boswell: Yes, Sir; you *tossed* and *gored* several persons.
> > Boswell   *Life of Johnson*
>
> Vaulting ambition, which *o'erleaps* itself.
> > Shakespeare   *Macbeth*
>
> Banners *flout* the sky.
> > Shakespeare   *Macbeth*
>
> And his answer *trickled* through my head.
> > Carroll   *Through the Looking-Glass*

Too many students, however, are willing to settle for those feeble "rubbish" verbs which not only fail to carry the action of the sentence forward but even add unnecessary length. You can nearly always improve sentences beginning "It is," "There is," or "There are" by lopping off the high-sounding but lazy and impersonal introductions:

Wordy	Improved
It is my plan to go through sorority rush.	I plan to go through sorority rush.

There is another problem we must consider.	We must consider another problem.
There are three reasons why Professor Billings says Whitman is "America's greatest poet."	Professor Billings lists three reasons for calling Whitman "America's greatest poet."

In addition, you should try to substitute specific action verbs for most (a) general verbs, (b) "state-of-being" verbs, and (c) passive verbs.

(a) *A general verb,* like a vague noun, is not easily defined because *general, specific, vague,* and *concrete* are relative terms rather than absolute qualities. For instance, the verb *rubbed* is more specific than the verb *touched* but less specific than the verb *stroked.* In principle, however, you should seek the most specific verb possible for the context.

General Verbs (Weak)	More Specific Verbs (Improved)
Mary Jo looked at my face.	Mary Jo studied my face.
The rock came through the window.	The rock crashed through the window.
The mud went through the cracks.	The mud oozed through the cracks.
The dragster ran down the track.	The dragster streaked down the track.
The Kid hit his opponent.	The Kid battered his opponent.
Martin fixed the desk top.	Martin sanded the desk top.

(b) *A linking verb* is any form of the verb *to be* (*be, am, is, are, was, were, been, being*) or another verb which means the same thing as some form of the verb *to be.*

Linking Verbs (Weak)	Action Verbs (Improved)
Bob was full of pity for the child. (*Was* is a form of the verb *to be.*)	Bob pitied the child. (Direct object is *child.*)

Donald grew weary of the dull jokes. (Sentence means *Donald was weary of the dull jokes.*)

Donald wearied of the dull jokes. (No direct object.)

American comic strips have become lacking in humor. (Sentence means *American comic strips are now lacking in humor.*)

American comic strips now lack humor. (Direct object is *humor.*)

(c) *A passive verb* occurs in a sentence in which the receiver of the action appears as the subject. The doer of the action is the object of a preposition (usually the preposition *by*).

Passive Verbs (Weak)	Active Verbs (Improved)
The party was attended by Nancy and Marge.	Nancy and Marge attended the party.
The movie was enjoyed by Aunt Kaye and me.	Aunt Kaye and I enjoyed the movie.
That question was missed by half the class.	Half the class missed that question.

The fact that the prepositional phrase may be either stated or understood complicates recognition of passive verbs.

Passive Verbs (Weak)	Active Verbs (Improved)
He was expelled for fairly obvious reasons. (*By the dean* is understood.)	The dean expelled him for fairly obvious reasons.
The books were counted three times. (*By us* is understood.)	We counted the books three times.
The glass of milk was drained. (*By Julie* is understood.)	Julie drained the glass of milk. (Direct object is *glass.*)
The paper was typed yesterday. (*By me* is understood.)	I typed the paper yesterday.

In general, the order of effectiveness for verbs, from weakest to strongest, is as follows: passive, linking, action with no direct object, and action with a direct object.

Hurriedly Hal ate the fried rice. (action verb with direct object—strongest)

Hal ate hurriedly. (action verb with no direct object—stronger still)

Hal's hurriedly-eaten dinner was fried rice. (linking verb—stronger)

The fried rice was eaten hurriedly by Hal. (passive verb—weakest)

Naturally, it will not be possible or even desirable to substitute action verbs for *all* passive verbs and linking verbs—or even for all general verbs which do not express a thought specifically. General verbs, as indicated above, are relative and therefore not easily recognized. And occasionally the elimination of a linking verb or passive verb will weaken the meaning or rhythm of a particular prose passage. As in most aspects of composition, therefore, your judgment is clearly more important than your strict observance of rules.

REPETITION, JARGON, AND GENERAL WORDINESS

Closely related to the overuse of adjectives and adverbs are other problems of style which weaken prose with excess wordage. *Repetition* saps vigor by boringly saying the same thing again.

Perhaps—particularly if you do not prepare an outline first—you will repeat whole sentences or ideas. More likely you will be tempted to repeat the meaning of a word in the adjoining word or phrase:

> red in color
> square in shape
> the metal gold
> absolutely unique
> chronologically in order of time
> in my opinion I believe
> beautiful in appearance
> promptly on time
> 4 P.M. in the afternoon
> empty vacuum
> nervous fear
> and etc.
> true fact
> paid professional
> unpaid amateur
> final end
> probing search
> worried anxiety
> collie dog
> solitary isolation
> repeat over again
> initially in the beginning
> predict beforehand
> eternally and forever
> tiny in size

Jargon blurs meaning by imitating high-sounding and semi-technical language. The elimination of these pompous and fuzzy words and phrases will nearly always improve sentence construction and meaning.

> in the case of
> the character of (referring to non-humans)
> the nature of
> as regards
> with regard to

in connection with
relative to
associated with
in respect of
as to whether

For a more detailed discussion of jargon, see *On the Art of Writing* by Sir Arthur Quiller-Couch (New York: G. P. Putnam's Sons, 1916).

General wordiness bores the reader by slowing down the process of communication. Although the average intelligent adult is willing to struggle to find the message in a piece of prose by a Tillich or a Locke or a Faulkner, most of us should assume that our ideas are not important enough for a reader to exert himself over.

Wordy	Improved
As for the majority of students, they wish that professors would make clear assignments.	Most students wish professors would make clear assignments.
Repect is a virtue that everyone should have and be taught.	Respect is a virtue that everyone should acquire.
During the time that she was in Europe, she visited her French relatives.	While she was in Europe, she visited her French relatives.
Joe's field of work is electrical engineering.	Joe is an electrical engineer.
Jane put in for a job which is in the country of Australia.	Jane applied for a job in Australia.
I didn't receive the scholarship because of the fact that Miss Simpson wouldn't recommend me.	I didn't receive the scholarship because Miss Simpson wouldn't recommend me.
While I was studying for my final in history, I kept wishing that Monty would call and that he would invite me to the Prom.	While studying for my history final, I kept wishing that Monty would call and invite me to the Prom.

For specific reasons, you may choose to break the rules in this discussion (in fact, any of the rules in this book). If you feel you need an extra word or two to achieve rhythm, balance, or emotional force, you should not feel bound by the principles discussed here. But unless you have a good reason for purposely ignoring them, you will find their observance will result in more direct and forceful prose.

Rules For Avoiding Wordiness and Vagueness

1. Do not substitute adjectives for exact nouns.
2. Use nouns which name things that can be seen, touched, heard, smelled, or tasted in preference to abstract nouns with similar meanings.
3. Do not use trite combinations of nouns and adjectives.
4. Crowd action into sentences with adjectives formed from vigorous verbs.
5. Do not substitute adverbs for vigorous verbs.
6. Avoid sentences beginning "It is," "There is," and "There are."
7. Replace linking verbs with action verbs.
8. Replace passive verbs with active verbs.
9. Avoid repetition, jargon, general wordiness.

Exercises

A. Vague Adjectives and Nouns

Rewrite the following sentences, substituting more exact expressions for the vague adjectives and nouns.

1. The little fast foreign car was parked near the garage.

2. The lady in charge of the party said we were going to play cards.

3. I went to the store to buy some food.

4. We hired someone who was well trained to help us select several pieces of furniture.

5. One of my brothers is unhappy because someone in a car ran over his pet.

6. He does things sometimes which are unfair.

7. The tree at the neighbor's house is lovely.

8. Much of the office was a mess.

9. A lady I know offered to help me with the sewing.

10. The floor covering doesn't look very good.

B. General Verbs

Find at least two specific verbs to replace the general verbs in each of
the following sentences.

1. The little boy (went) _____ to school.
2. The sick girl (went) _____ to school.
3. The frantic teacher (went) _____ to school.
4. The old janitor (went) _____ to school.
5. The cat (ran) _____ from the dog.
6. The cat (ran) _____ after the mouse.
7. The fog (came) _____ down from the
    mountain.
8. The driver of the other car (looked) _____
    at me.
9. Jean (put) _____ the dishes on the table.
10. Jackie (gave) _____ me the ball.
11. The hail (came) _____ down on the roof.
12. The speaker (talked) _____ for hours.
13. The grass (grew) _____ through the weeds.
14. Mark (ate) _____ his dinner.
15. I (held) _____ the dog.

C. Action and Active Verbs

Rewrite the following sentences, substituting action and active verbs for linking and passive verbs.

1. Many anxious moments are spent by secretaries who don't keep their files current.

2. As we drove along the freeway, a sign was seen announcing Milton's new fish restaurant.

3. The teacher's comments on my theme were not read until today.

4. He had become sickened at the bloodshed.

5. Joan was not introduced to the class by the teacher for three days.

6. Maxine was fearful about her little sister's reaction to the war movie.

7. I did not turn in the assignment on time because unforeseen difficulties were encountered.

8. The letter was mailed by me on October 1.

9. I was hopeful that his reaction to my letter would be good.

10. The dog was taken to the hospital after he had been hit by the truck.

11. The waste basket was emptied, but still the missing ring was not found.

12. Lorraine was desirous of seeing her name in print.

13. The pictures in Eric's room were hung by him before Christmas.

14. Matt was missed by his sister when she was in attendance at her first kindergarten class.

15. Often time is wasted by members of an audience who are interrupters during a speech.

D. Wordiness and Vagueness

Rewrite the following sentences to eliminate unnecessary words and vague concepts.

1. With regard to space exploration, the Russians claim to be ahead of the country of the United States.

2. In the case of Pam, she had high grades academically but did not engage in extra curricular activities outside of school.

3. The entire book is depressing in nature, but I venture to say that people will read it anyway.

4. In the modern world of today no one chooses styles which are flattering to him or to her.

5. During the time that I was in Canada, I visited Banff, Lake Louise, Victoria, and etc.

6. The character of most of the houses on the street is quaint and charming.

7. In my own mind I thought that the dinner tasted terrible.

8. I plan to attend an institution of higher learning to study for my life's work in the field of dentistry.

9. I visited a psychologist concerning the matter of leaving home and striking out for myself in some work along the line of electronics.

10. To admit of failure in connection with academic performance in the instance of history was a condition which Laurel could not persuade herself about.

11. Despite the fact that it was 4:30 A.M. in the morning, Mark was punctually dressed on time to go fishing.

12. The soldiers came down the street in absolutely parallel lines.

E. Theme Assignment

Using one of the topics below, write a theme of 500-600 words, paying particular attention to concise and concrete use of language.

Advice for a friend
If I could change myself
Family life twenty years from now
The future of American education

Step 11. How to Use Figurative Language

Another kind of flapdoodle occurs when a word, phrase, sentence, or passage interrupts the flow of communication by calling attention to itself. But the ability to recognize words that are too showy and images that are too startling often takes years of conscious effort and is always more easily applied to someone else's writing than your own. That is one reason why even professional writers must struggle with editors and critics before and after their work gets into print.

It might be argued, for instance, that Abraham Lincoln was guilty of flapdoodle when he began the Gettysburg Address by saying "Fourscore and seven years ago" instead of simply "Eighty-seven years ago . . ." This is really an overblown phrase which could not be defended at all except for the ear-catching rhythm of the construction. Lincoln's wide and careful reading from early childhood had produced a keen ear which was sensitive to the rhythms and sounds of prose. In the Gettysburg Address, all of which is written with the same attention to prose sounds, the introductory phrase is appropriate. In another piece of writing it would not be. Lincoln therefore demonstrates flair (discriminating taste) and not flapdoodle (nonsense), but he shows us how closely related the two are.

Flair in writing is often associated with poetry, and for this reason skillful and sensitive prose passages—such as certain ones by Herman Melville, John Steinbeck, or William Faulkner, for instance—are often said to be "poetic." The techniques of poetry are not necessarily different from those of prose, but they are much more carefully distilled. Poetry is a tightly-compressed form of communication, and each word in a poem must be chosen wisely in order to advance the author's meaning. You can therefore sometimes recognize prose techniques more quickly if you study good poetry or terse prose like that of the King James Bible.

DEVELOPING YOUR SENSES

Although exposition (that is, explanation) is largely concerned with seeing with the mind, the mind relies on the impressions of the five senses: sight, sound, touch, smell, and taste. Thus by recording sensory impressions for your reader, you can often make his task of grappling with your explanation easier. For instance, you might say that Jane looked sick, but if you describe her protruding cheek bones, her drooping eyelids, and the pale yellow circle around her mouth, the reader is more likely to be convinced. Or perhaps you can offer more than mere visual impression. Perhaps you can describe the cold, dank feeling of her skin or the wheezy sound to her breathing so that the impressions of touch and sound give reinforcement to what is seen.

Possibly because they experience physical sensations more keenly than the rest of us, poets recognize the importance of sensory description in conveying an idea to the reader. It would be impossible to find a page of good poetry that did not contain passages which appeal to the senses. Some brief examples follow:

Sight

As creeping ivy clings to wood or stone,
And hides the ruin that it feeds upon.
Cowper   Progress of Error

So when the sun in bed,
Curtain'd with cloudy red,
Pillows his chin upon an orient wave.
Milton   Hymn. On the Morning of
Christ's Nativity

Out went the taper as she hurried in;
Its little smoke, in pallid moonshine, died.
Keats   The Eve of Saint Agnes

Fast fading violets cover'd up in leaves.

> Keats   *Ode to a Nightingale*

And those thin clouds above, in flakes and bars,
That give away their motion to the stars.

> Coleridge   *Dejection: an Ode*

Passing the yellow-spear'd wheat, every grain from its shroud
in the dark-brown fields uprising.

> Whitman   *When Lilacs Last in the
> Door-Yard Bloom'd*

With floods of the yellow gold of the gorgeous, indolent, sink-
ing sun, burning, expanding the air.

> Whitman   *When Lilacs Last in the
> Door-Yard Bloom'd*

While ravening clouds, the burial clouds, in black masses
spreading.

> Whitman   *On the Beach*

Four beating wings, two beaks, a swirling mass tight grappling,
In tumbling turning clustering loops, straight downward
falling.

> Whitman   *The Dalliance of the
> Eagles*

When all at once I saw a crowd,
A host, of golden daffodils;
Beside the lake, beneath the trees,
Fluttering and dancing in the breeze.

> Wordsworth   *I Wandered Lonely
> as a Cloud*

Sound

The curfew tolls the knell of parting day,
   The lowing herd wind slowly o'er the lea.

> Gray   *Elegy Written in a Country
> Churchyard*

A solitary shriek, the bubbling cry
Of some strong swimmer in his agony.

> Byron   *Don Juan*

Her rich attire creeps rustling to her knees.

> Keats   *The Eve of Saint Agnes*

Then in a wailful choir the small gnats mourn.

> Keats   *To Autumn*

And let your silver chime
Move in melodious time;
And let the base of heav'ns deep organ blow.
Milton   *Hymn. On the Morning of*
Christ's Nativity

The poplars are fell'd, farewell to the shade
And the whispering sound of the cool colonnade.
Cowper   *The Popular Field*

To hear the lark begin his flight,
And singing startle the dull night.
Milton   *L'Allegro*

The murmurous haunt of flies on summer eves.
Keats   *Ode to a Nightingale*

Solitary, the thrush,

. . .

Sings by himself a song.
Song of the bleeding throat!
Whitman   *When Lilacs Last in the*
Door-Yard Bloom'd

As low and wailing, yet clear the notes, rising and falling,
  flooding the night.
Whitman   *When Lilacs Last in the*
Door-Yard Bloom'd

Touch

With aching hands, and bleeding feet
  We dig and heap, lay stone on stone;
We bear the burden and the heat
  Of the long day, and wish 'twere none.
Arnold   *Morality*

O Love, O fire! once he drew
With one long kiss my whole soul thro'
My lips, as sunlight drinketh dew.
Tennyson   *Fatima*

This living hand, now warm and capable
Of earnest grasping, would, if it were cold
And in the icy silence of the tomb,
So haunt thy days and chill thy dreaming nights
That thou wouldst wish thine own heart dry of blood.
Keats   *Lines to Fanny Brawne*

Batter my heart, three person'd God.

> Donne   *Holy Sonnets*

The spider's touch how exquisitely fine!
Feels at each thread, and lives along the line.

> Pope   *An Essay on Man*

On the white shore dripping, dripping, suck'd in by the sand;
. . .
Moist tears from the eyes of a muffled head.

> Whitman   *Tears*

And a thousand slimy things
      Lived on.

> Coleridge   *The Ancient Mariner*

Fill all thy bones with aches.

> Shakespeare   *The Tempest*

Burning with high hope, shall moulder cold and low.

> Byron   *Childe Harold*

I am the hounded slave, I wince at the bite of the dogs,
Hell and despair are upon me, crack and again
      crack the marksmen;
I clutch the rails of the fence, my gore drips, thinn'd with the
      ooze of my skin.

> Whitman   *Song of Myself*

Taste

Then to the spicy nut-brown ale.

> Milton   *L'Allegro*

O, for a draught of vintage! that hath been
Cool'd a long age in the deep-delved earth.

> Keats   *Ode to a Nightingale*

The savoury pulp they chew, and in the rind
Still as they thirsted scooped the brimming stream.

> Milton   *Paradise Lost*

Chew'd bitter ashes, which th' offended taste
With spattering noise rejected.

> Milton   *Paradise Lost*

The bud may have a bitter taste,
      But sweet will be the flow'r.

> Cowper   *Olney Hymns*

The fathers have eaten sour grapes, and the children's teeth
    are set on edge.
Ezekiel 18:2

Things sweet to taste prove in digestion sour.
Shakespeare   *King Richard II*

Give them great meals of beef and iron and steel,
    they will eat like wolves and fight like devils.
Shakespeare   *King Henry V*

Like a summer-dried fountain,
    When our need was the sorest.
Scott   *The Lady of the Lake*

Like to the apples on the Dead Sea's shore,
All ashes to the taste.
Byron   *Childe Harold*

Smell

A steam of rich distill'd perfumes.
Milton   *Comus*

Yet the lilac, with mastering odor, holds me.
Whitman   *When Lilacs Last in the
Door-Yard Bloom'd*

A mile of warm sea-scented beach.
Browning   *Meeting at Night*

    Here's flowers for you;
Hot lavender, mints, savory, marjoram.
Shakespeare   *The Winter's Tale*

And the woodbine spices are wafted abroad,
    And the musk of the rose is blown.
Tennyson   *Maud*

Groves whose rich trees wept odorous gums and balm.
Milton   *Paradise Lost*

Drows'd with the fume of poppies.
Keats   *To Autumn*

Where blossomed many an incense-bearing tree.
Coleridge   *Kubla Khan*

    I have rather live
With cheese and garlic in a windmill far.
Shakespeare   *King Henry IV* Part I

By summer's ripening breath.
Shakespeare   *Romeo and Juliet*

Figures of Speech

Another device commonly associated with poetry is the use of figures of speech, that is, words and phrases which carry meanings beyond their literal ones. Possibly without realizing it, you use figures of speech in conversation every day. You talk about *polishing apples, splitting hairs, putting your feet in your mouth, brainstorming*, or *getting a cold shoulder* without ever meaning exactly what you say, yet with little fear of being misunderstood by your friends.

In conversation you seldom have time to compose original figures of speech to replace worn-out expressions such as these, but in writing you should take greater care to make your words work for you in the best ways that they possibly can. Again by studying lines from good poets you can see how figures of speech, when appropriately used, add depth of meaning to the poets' ideas.

Metaphor (MET-a-fer)

A metaphor is an implied comparison in which one thing is spoken of in terms of something else. Metaphors are extremely valuable in making an abstract idea more clear by associating it with something concrete, familiar, or vivid.

Thou god of our idolatry, the press.
> Cowper   *Progress of Error*

Remorse, the fatal egg by pleasure laid.
> Cowper   *Progress of Error*

The soul's dark cottage, batter'd and decay'd
Lets in new light through chinks that time has made.
> Waller   *On the Foregoing Divine Poems*

Eating the bitter bread of banishment.
> Shakespeare   *King Richard II*

Entangled in the cobwebs of the schools.
> Cowper   *The Task*

A child said *What is the grass?* fetching it to one
   with full hands;
. . .
Or I guess it is the handkerchief of the Lord.
> Whitman   *Song of Myself*

O for a beaker full of the warm South.

>   Keats   *Ode to a Nightingale*

Man is the shuttle, to whose winding quest
And passage through these looms
God order'd motion, but ordain'd no rest.

>   Vaughan   *Silex Scintillans*

They shall splash at a ten-league canvas with brushes of
>   comets' hair.

>   Kipling   *When Earth's*
>   *Last Picture*

A livelier emerald twinkles in the grass,
A purer sapphire melts into the sea.

>   Tennyson   *Maud*

Simile (SIM-i-lee)

A simile is a direct comparison of two things, usually employing *like* or *as*.

Thy words are like a cloud of winged snakes.

>   Shelley   *Prometheus Unbound*

Drive my dead thoughts over the universe
Like withered leaves to quicken a new birth!

>   Shelley   *Ode to the West Wind*

And like a dying lady, lean and pale,
Who totters forth, wrapped in a gauzy veil.

>   Shelley   *The Waning Moon*

Hell is a city much like London—
A populous and smoky city.

>   Shelley   *Peter Bell the Third*

My heart is like an apple-tree
Whose boughs are bent with thickset fruit.

>   Christina Rossetti   *A Birthday*

How, like a moth, the simple maid
>   Still plays about the flame!

>   Gay   *The Beggar's Opera*

Prison'd in a parlour snug and small,
Like bottled wasps upon a southern wall.

>   Cowper   *Retirement*

As flies to wanton boys, are we to the gods:
They kill us for their sport.

>   Shakespeare   *King Lear*

I am as vigilant as a cat to steal cream.

Shakespeare   *King Henry IV,* Part 1

Their ranks are breaking thin clouds before a Biscay gale.

Macaulay   *The Battle of Naseby*

Hyperbole (hy-PER-boe-lee)

Hyperbole is the use of exaggeration or overstatement which is not intended to be taken literally. It may be used for emphasis, for humor, or for poetic intensity.

Studios let me sit,
And hold high converse with the mighty dead.

Thomson   *The Seasons*

Here once the embattled farmers stood,
And fired the shot heard round the world.

Emerson   *Hymn Sung at the Completion of the Concord Monument*

Who steals my purse steals trash.

Shakespeare   *Othello*

He doth nothing but talk of his horse.

Shakespeare   *The Merchant of Venice*

There's nothing serious in mortality.

Shakespeare   *Macbeth*

I am large, I contain multitudes.

Whitman   *Song of Myself*

Stop this day and night with me, and you shall possess
the origin of all poems.

Whitman   *Song of Myself*

With the twirl of my tongue I encompass worlds, and
volumes of worlds.

Whitman   *Song of Myself*

The orchestra whirls me wider than Uranus flies.

Whitman   *Song of Myself*

There was a child went forth every day;
And the first object he look'd upon, that object he became.

Whitman   *There Was a Child Went Forth*

Personification

Personification is the assigning of human qualities to inanimate objects or abstract ideas. Of all the figures of speech listed here, it is by far the most difficult to handle well, for it easily leads to the flapdoodle of sentimentality. Most English teachers discourage even their advanced students from using it, but it is included here so that you can recognize it when you see it.

> Things are in the saddle,
>   And ride mankind.
> > Emerson   *Ode, Inscribed to*
> > *W. H. Channing*

> For evil news rides post, while good news baits.
> > Milton   *Samson Agonistes*

> Truth forever on the scaffold, Wrong forever on the throne.
> > Lowell   *The Present Crisis*

> Into the jaws of Death,
> Into the mouth of Hell.
> > Tennyson   *The Charge of the*
> > *Light Brigade*

> The slings and arrows of outrageous fortune.
> > Shakespeare   *Hamlet*

> When Faith is kneeling by his bed of death.
> > Drayton   *Idea*

> But such a tide as moving seems asleep.
> > Tennyson   *Crossing the Bar*

> The dirty nurse, Experience.
> > Tennyson   *The Idylls of the King*

> For the sure-enwinding arms of cool-enfolding death.
> > Whitman   *When Lilacs Last in the*
> > *Door-Yard Bloom'd*

> And now it seems to me the beautiful uncut hair of graves.
> > Whitman   *Song of Myself*

Irony

Irony is a figure of speech in which the author's meaning is quite different—sometimes even the opposite—from what he literally says. As a technique of humor and satire (see p. 171) it occurs more frequently in prose than poetry, and the following examples are all taken from prose literature.

> But Tom Sawyer he hunted me up and said he was going to start a band of robbers, and I might join if I would go back to the widow and be respectable.
>
> Twain   *The Adventures of*
> *Huckleberry Finn*

> Whoever has lived long enough to find out what life is, knows how deep a debt of gratitude we owe to Adam, the first great benefactor of our race. He brought death into the world.
>
> Twain   *Pudd'nhead Wilson's*
> *Calendar*

> When I reflect upon the number of disagreeable people who I know have gone to a better world, I am moved to lead a different life.
>
> Twain   *Pudd'nhead Wilson's*
> *Calendar*

> July 4. Statistics show that we lose more fools on this day than in all the other days of the year put together. This proves, by the number left in stock, that one Fourth of July per year is now inadequate, the country has grown so.
>
> Twain   *Pudd'nhead Wilson's*
> *Calendar*

> The English are mentioned in the Bible: Blessed are the meek, for they shall inherit the earth.
>
> Twain   *Pudd'nhead Wilson's*
> *New Calendar*

> To succeed in the other trades, capacity must be shown; in the law, concealment of it will do.
>
> Twain   *Pudd'nhead Wilson's*
> *New Calendar*

> Better be killed than frightened to death.
>
> Surtees   *Mr. Facey Romford's*
> *Hounds*

> Thinking that life would be very pleasant if it were not for its enjoyments.
>
> Surtees   *Mr. Facey Romford's*
> *Hounds*

I never saw, heard, nor read, that the clergy were beloved in any nation where Christianity was the religion of the country. Nothing can render them popular but some degree of persecution.

Swift   *Thoughts on Religion*

Promises and pie-crust are made to be broken.

Swift   *Polite Conversation*

Formerly textbooks listed many other figures of speech, but numerous classifications are not helpful because categories tend to overlap. In the lists above, for instance, most of the entries under *personification* and *hyperbole* could also be placed under metaphor; and distinctions between *hyperbole* and *irony* are often debatable. The important thing to remember is that figurative language—or expressions that are not intended to be taken literally—can make writing colorful when handled well.

PROBLEMS WITH FIGURES OF SPEECH

Having now become aware of the depth and vigor which good figures of speech can add to composition, you should also remember the earlier warning against flapdoodle, for nothing gives away second-rate prose and poetry as quickly as ineffective figures. Poor figures of speech are those which are (1) mixed, (2) trite, (3) unnatural, or (4) habitual.

(1) *Mixed figures of speech* result when two or more unrelated concepts are combined in a single sentence or paragraph. The figures may startle the reader, but probably not in the way the writer intends:

His milk of human kindness was the key to his success.

The campaign is going so swimmingly that Harper is certain he will carry the election.

One way to smoke out a crook is to give him enough rope to hang himself.

She gave me an icy stare which really burned me up.

The secretary will dig her own grave if she tries to fill the president's shoes.

For some people college is a bed of roses, but it usually separates the sheep from the goats.

I sat on needles and pins waiting for the butterflies to leave my stomach.

(2) *Trite figures of speech* are those which have been dulled by sheer banditry. Stolen so often by later writers, the following figures of speech no longer give off any luster—either for the careless thieves or for the exacting authors who originally coined them.

The sight of you is good for sore eyes.
> Swift   *Polite Conversation*

She has more goodness in her little finger, than he has in his whole body.
> Swift   *Polite Conversation*

He was sure it would rain cats and dogs.
> Swift   *Polite Conversation*

You've a darned long row to hoe.
> Lowell   *The Biglow Papers*

This is the way to kill a wife with kindness.
> Shakespeare   *The Taming of the Shrew*

Misery acquaints a man with strange bedfellows.
> Shakespeare   *The Tempest*

He hath eaten me out of house and home.
> Shakespeare   *King Henry IV*, Part II

Hitch your wagon to a star.
> Emerson   *Society and Solitude*

He uses language that would make your hair curl.
> Gilbert   *Ruddigore*

(3) *Unnatural figures of speech* occur when the writer injects figurative expressions which are too formal, too pompous, too humorous, too serious, too slangy, or too ridiculous for the passages in which they appear.

The judge shifted his weight and gave the defendant a quizzical look which clearly indicated that he didn't dig the testimony.

Slowly, slowly Jake bent the iron bar, his huge biceps twitching like the wings of a butterfly balancing on a single blade of grass.

Like mighty Zeus calling a council of the Gods, the teacher rang the bell for the end of recess.

The pages of the comic book were torn and smudged and bore pencil marks that looked like the windings of a great river feeling its way to the ocean.

(4) *Habitual figures of speech* weaken composition because the reader does not have time to respond to one before moving on to the next. As a general rule, however, similes are the most irritating of all figures of speech when they are overworked because the repeated sounds of *like* and *as* grind the ear even when passages are read silently.

More Poetic Devices: Rhyme, Assonance, Alliteration, Onomatopoeia

Sometimes identified as figures of speech, rhyme, assonance, alliteration, and onomatopoeia do not meet the definition (i.e., meanings which words and phrases carry beyond their literal ones) as clearly as the kinds of figures discussed above.

Rhyme and assonance are more commonly used in poetry than in prose where they often become forced and inappropriate. The exceptions, of course, would be advertising gimmicks, political slogans, titles, or headlines which for some reason must attract immediate attention. *I like Ike,* for instance, helped to elect a president of the United States because it is not only brief but because it contains both rhyme and assonance. *Rhyme* (two or more words ending with a syllable containing the same vowel and consonant sounds) occurs in *like* and *Ike*. *Assonance* (two or more words ending with a syllable containing the same vowel sound) occurs in all three words.

Alliteration is the device of beginning two or more words with the same sound. Like rhyme and assonance, it is more commonly encountered in poetry than prose.

How silver-sweet sound lovers' tongues by night.
Shakespeare   *Romeo and Juliet*

Five miles meandering with a mazy motion.
Coleridge   *Kubla Khan*

Destructive, damnable, deceitful woman.
Otway   *The Orphan*

Bleak blows the blast.

> Canning   *The Friend of Humanity*
> *and the Knife-Grinder*

He clasps the crag with crooked hands.

> Tennyson   *The Eagle*

Whereat, with blade, with bloody blameful blade,
He bravely broach'd his boiling bloody breast.

> Shakespeare   *A Midsummer*
> *Night's Dream*

Strange sounds along the chancel pass'd.

> Scott   *The Lay of the Last Minstrel*

Onomatopoeia (on-uh-mah-tuh-PEE-a) is the device by which
words imitate the sounds they name. Useful both in poetry and
prose, it calls for careful attention to what is being said and the use
of vivid action verbs. After studying the examples below, turn again
to the list of sound descriptions on p. 124 to see how many of them
rely on the use of onomatopoeia.

Bang-whang-whang goes the drum, tootle-to-tootle the fife.

> Browning   *Up at a Villa—*
> *Down in the City*

And the brass will crash,
    And the trumpet bray.

> Gilbert   *The Mikado*

We hissed along the polished ice.

> Wordsworth   *Influence of*
> *Natural Objects*

How the hungry lion roars,
    And the wolf behowls the moon.

> Shakespeare   *A Midsummer*
> *Night's Dream*

With twelve great shocks of sound, the shameless noon
Was clash'd and hammer'd from a hundred towers.

> Tennyson   *Godiva*

The mellow lin-lan-lone of evening bells.

> Tennyson   *Far-Far-Away*

You undertone of rivers, roar of pouring cataracts;
You sounds from distant guns, with galloping cavalry!

> Whitman   *Proud Music of the Storm*

And hush'd with buzzing night-flies to thy slumber.

> Shakespeare *King Henry IV* Part II

And every soul, it passed me by,
Like the whizz of my cross-bow.

> Coleridge *The Ancient Mariner*

Where the mocking-bird sounds his delicious gurgles, cackles,
screams, weeps.

> Whitman *Song of Myself*

By making effective use of the kinds of sensory description and figures of speech illustrated above in your next expository theme, you will find that your prose will take on rich, expressive qualities.

Exercises

A. Identification of Poetic Devices

The following prose passages from *The Adventures of Huckleberry Finn* by Mark Twain contain many devices considered "poetic." Underline all the evidences of sensory description and the figures of speech. Identify what the devices are in the margin at right.

1. When I got there it was all still and Sunday-like, and hot and sunshiny; the hands was gone to the fields; and there was them kind of faint dronings of bugs and flies in the air that makes it seem so lonesome and like everybody's dead and gone; and if a breeze fans along and quivers the leaves it makes you feel mournful, because you feel like it's spirits whispering—spirits that's been dead ever so many years—and you always think they're talking about *you*. As a general thing it makes a body wish *he* was dead, too, and done with it all.

2. We spread the blankets inside for a carpet, and eat our dinner in there. We put all the other things handy at the back of the cavern. Pretty soon it darkened up, and begun to thunder and lighten; so the birds was right about it. Directly it begun to rain, and **it rained** like all fury, too, and I ne**ver see the** wind blow so. It was one of **these** regular summer storms. It would get so dark that it looked all blue-black outside, and lovely; and the rain would thrash along by so thick that the trees off a little ways looked dim and spider-webby; and here would come a blast of wind that would bend the trees down and

turn up the pale underside of the leaves; and then a perfect ripper of a gust would follow along and set the branches to tossing their arms as if they was just wild; and next, when it was just about the bluest and blackest—fst! it was as bright as glory, and you'd have a little glimpse of tree-tops a-plunging about away off yonder in the storm, hundreds of yards further than you could see before; dark as sin again in a second, and now you'd hear the thunder let go with an awful crash, and then go rumbling, grumbling, tumbling, down the sky towards the under side of the world, like rolling empty barrels down-stairs—where it's long stairs and they bounce a good deal, you know.

3. A little smoke couldn't be noticed now, so we would take some fish off the lines and cook up a hot breakfast. And afterwards we would watch the lonesomeness of the river, and kind of lazy along, and by and by lazy off to sleep. Wake up by and by, and look to see what done it, and maybe see a steamboat coughing along upstream, so far off towards the other side you couldn't tell nothing about her only whether she was a stern-wheel or side-wheel; then for about an hour there wouldn't be nothing to hear nor nothing to see— just solid lonesomeness. Next you'd see a raft sliding by, away off yonder, and maybe a galoot on it chopping, because they're most always doing it on a raft; you'd see the ax flash and come down— you don't hear nothing; you see that ax go up again, and by the time it's above the man's head then you hear the k'chunk—it had took all that time to come over the water. So we would put

in the day, lazying around, listening to
the stillness. Once there was a thick fog,
and the rafts and things that went by
was beating tin pans so the steamboats
wouldn't run over them. A scow or a
raft went by so close we could hear
them talking and cussing and laughing
—heard them plain; but we couldn't see
no sign of them; it made you feel
crawly; it was like spirits carrying on
that way in the air.

B. Theme Assignment

Using one of the topics below, write a descriptive theme of 400-500 words which appeals to as many of the five senses as possible. Limit your subject to one specific place.

A restaurant	A thunder shower	A hospital
A laundry	A ski resort	A garage
A wedding reception	A reducing salon	A mountain lake
A newspaper office	A beauty parlor	An artist's studio
A supermarket	A classroom	An outdoor barbecue
A mortuary	A florist shop	A hunting camp
A clambake		

Step 12. How to Make Quotable Quotes

Why is it that some passages from literature are long remembered whereas others—equally true or thoughtful—are not? Why, for instance, do we quote so frequently from Benjamin Franklin, who as an author did not express ideas which were very original or very deep? Or why do we remember Shakespeare's plays and not the earlier versions of the same stories? Why can we recite the Gettysburg Address by Lincoln but have no idea what Edward Everett Hale had to say on the same occasion? And why do we still cling to the familiar scriptures from the King James version of the Bible when we have access to far more accurate translations?

Beyond the poetic devices discussed in Step 11 are the less showy but more important elements of style which distinguish good writing from satisfactory writing. Or in student terms, these are the elements which distinguish *A* and *B* themes from the adequate but uninspired *C* paper. Among them are clarity, consistency, proper subordination, variety, emphasis, and balance.

CLARITY

Clear writing reflects good manners, for no writer who cares about his reader will want to confuse him. But despite how obvious and simple a principle clarity seems, it requires determination. For one thing, it requires a knowledge of grammar and a willingness to admit that a weak construction can muddy intended meaning.

Confusing	Clear
He decided to finish law school when he was in bed with the flu.	When he was in bed with the flu, he decided to finish law school.
If you have any children, please send in the enclosed envelope.	Please send information about your children in the enclosed envelope.
As I reached for the dog's bone, it bit me.	The dog bit me as I reached for its bone.
Correcting the themes, coffee was spilled all over the papers.	Correcting the themes, the teacher spilled coffee all over the themes.

For another thing, clarity requires an awareness of the audience for whom the material is intended.

First Grade Primer	College Textbook
See the girl. She lives far, far away. See her dress. Her dress is not like yours.	The termination of the twin concepts of empire and colonialism have resulted in a power vacuum which the U.N. has been unable to fill.

For another, it requires constant attention to the overall thesis and pattern. And finally, clarity depends upon the willingness to re-read and revise.

But clarity is not enough. It is merely the minimum standard all writing should meet. To write distinguished prose the student must employ the increasingly subtle elements of style discussed hereafter.

CONSISTENCY

Exposition which contains unnecessary shifts in person, voice, tense, and level of usage may lack clarity. More commonly, however, it simply annoys the reader and forces him to dismiss the writer as incompetent.

Inconsistent Person

Because most shifts in person involve the use of the second person pronoun *you,* many teachers will instruct students never to use this word in their themes.

Inconsistent	Consistent
When freshmen arrive for college registration, you must stand in line for nearly two days.	When freshmen arrive for college registration, they must stand in line for nearly two days.
I have always wished I had studied dancing because you wouldn't feel so heavy-footed when you go out on dates.	I have always wished I had studied dancing so I wouldn't feel so heavy-footed when I go out on dates.
The dog lapped the water wildly, for you always get parched after running so fast.	The dog lapped the water wildly, for he was always parched after running so fast.

Inconsistent Voice

Inconsistent	Consistent
After we took our seats, the conductor was seen coming down the aisle.	After we took our seats, we saw the conductor coming down the aisle.
Jill went to school before her bed had been made.	Jill went to school before she made her bed.
The report was made by Douglas and me as soon as we entered the committee room.	Douglas and I submitted the report as soon as we entered the committee room.

The passive voice causes further problems when you are giving directions because you are likely to become involved in shifts of person as well as shifts of voice.

Inconsistent	Consistent
Separate the egg; then the egg white should be beaten until it stands in peaks.	Separate the egg; then beat the egg white until it stands in peaks.
You enter the park from 7th Street, and the route to the lion cage will be found to be shorter.	You enter the park from 7th Street, and you will find the route to the lion cage is shorter.
Don't apply the second coat until the first is completely dry, or the paint cannot be put on smoothly.	Don't apply the second coat until the first is completely dry, or you cannot put the paint on smoothly.

Inconsistent Tense

Although the context will justify occasional changes in verb tense, many students shift tenses thoughtlessly.

Inconsistent	Consistent
After he watched the Senate in session, Craig decides to enter politics.	After he watched the Senate in session, Craig decided to enter politics.
Rosemary and I plan to get married next month. She was my only girl friend for three years.	Rosemary and I plan to get married next month. She has been my only girl friend for three years.
Milton packs his bag and leaves home after his father scolded him.	Milton packs his bag and leaves home after his father scolds him.

Inconsistent Level of Usage

Formal and informal expressions may be appropriate on different occasions but should not be mixed within a single sentence, paragraph, or composition.

Inconsistent	Consistent
The implicit demands of suburban life compelled	The implicit demands of suburban life compelled

him after five anguished years to do himself in.	him after five anguished years to commit suicide.
I'm real enthused about my invitation to participate on the panel discussing Michener's theory of the evolution of Yahweh.	I am very enthusiastic about my invitation to participate on the panel discussing Michener's theory of the evolution of Yahweh.
The first violinist loused up the mood when he halted the orchestra in the second movement.	The first violinist destroyed the mood when he halted the orchestra in the second movement.

PROPER SUBORDINATION

Another common error in student writing is the construction of sentences in which important ideas and unimportant ideas are treated equally or upside down. Some poor techniques are (1) piling up of simple sentences, (2) piling up of coordinate clauses, (3) piling up of dependent clauses, (4) using "and" or "but" before subordinating conjunctions, or (5) putting main ideas in dependent constructions.

(1) *Piling up of simple sentences* results in jerky, immature prose of the kind we read in first grade primers:

I like to ski. Last winter I fell down. I broke my leg in two places. The doctor put me in an uncomfortable cast. I couldn't ski the rest of the season.

This kind of stop-and-start writing bogs the reader down not only because of the unnecessary punctuation but because he must seek out the important ideas which the writer has failed to signal for him.

(2) *Piling up of coordinate clauses* results in the breathless kind of reporting that the young child uses in trying to tell everything he knows at once:

I like to ski, but last winter I fell down, and I broke my leg in two places. The doctor put me in an uncomfortable cast, and I couldn't ski the rest of the season.

This kind of writing leaves the reader panting as well as the writer, for neither seems to be moving anywhere, just running and running.

(3) *Piling up of dependent clauses* seems equally purposeless, for each new clause must lean upon the one which precedes it:

> I like skiing which I did last winter until I fell down when I broke my leg which had to be put in a cast which was uncomfortable.

(4) *Using "and" or "but" before subordinating conjunctions* is usually incorrect grammatically as well as ineffective stylistically.

> I like skiing and which I did last winter until I fell down. I broke my leg and which had to be put in an uncomfortable cast.

(5) *Putting main ideas in dependent constructions* results in upside-down logic.

> When I broke my leg, I was skiing.

This sentence might be appropriate in certain contexts, but the writer probably means *While I was skiing, I broke my leg.*

Rather than settling for one of the five poor sentence constructions listed above, you should decide upon the single idea (or possibly two ideas) you want to emphasize and then place the other closely-related elements in some kind of dependent construction: adverb, adjective, dependent clause, prepositional phrase, participial phrase, or infinitive phrase.

Not subordinated	Subordinated	Constructions
The dog snarled. The dog came after me. The dog bit me. The bite hurt.	[Snarling], the dog came after me and gave me a [painful] bite.	Participle Adjective
I finished my history assignment, and I was worn out, and I went to bed.	[After finishing my history assignment], I was so worn out [that I went to bed].	Prepositional phrase containing gerund Dependent clause
He has been away six months. He hasn't written. I am unhappy.	I am unhappy [because he hasn't written] [in the six months] [that he has been away].	Dependent clause Prepositional phrase Dependent clause

Of all the possible dependent constructions, you may find the participle to be the most useful and yet one of the most difficult to master. As explained on p. 105, a participle is an adjective formed from a verb. Present participles always end in *ing*. Past participles frequently end in *d, ed, t, n,* or *en*. Participles may appear alone or within phrases.

Not subordinated	Subordinated	Participle used
Patti showed us her play house. It was made by her Uncle Fred.	Patti showed us her play house made by her Uncle Fred.	*Made*—past
The bird was cooing at dawn. It awakened us.	Cooing at dawn, the bird awakened us.	*Cooing*—present
The woman was angered by the salesgirl. She left the store.	Angered by the salesgirl, the woman left the store.	*Angered*—past
Donna was frightened by the storm. She was instinctively ducking the thunder. She ran across the field.	Frightened by the storm and instinctively ducking the thunder, Donna ran across the field.	*Frightened*—past *Ducking*—present

Notice that the verb drops its helping verb when it becomes an adjective (participle).

VARIETY

The English language, unlike many other languages, presents such endless possibilities of word order that teachers often wonder why students ever must be reminded to vary their sentence structure. Often, however, students become so committed to the normal sentence order that they feel they have produced a radical change if they begin an occasional sentence with a prepositional phrase or a dependent clause. Certainly you should keep your audience clearly in mind (*e.g.,* grade school children, high school seniors, non-professional adults, college graduates) and produce sentence lengths and sentence patterns which your readers can handle. But even young children can cope with some variety. And for intelligent adult readers the need for sentence variety is as real as the need for menu variety. Undoubtedly you will agree that a menu of pork chops, mashed potatoes, and carrots—satisfying as it may be—can get fairly tiresome if served three meals a day.

SENTENCE PATTERNS COMMONLY USED BY STUDENTS

Simple Sentences (Normal Order)

Walt ate.   (subject, verb)

Walt ate slowly.   (subject, verb, adverb)

Walt ate the turkey.   (subject, verb, direct object)

Walt ate the turkey slowly.   (subject, verb, direct object, adverb)

Walt ate the turkey in a hurry.   (subject, verb, direct object, prepositional phrase)

Walt and his mother ate the turkey.   (subject, subject, verb, direct object)

Walt ate and enjoyed the turkey.   (subject, verb, verb, direct object)

Walt ate the turkey and the pie.   (subject, verb, direct object, direct object)

Turkey and pie are basic to Thanksgiving dinner.   (subject, subject, verb, subjective complement, prepositional phrase)

Compound Sentence

Walt ate the turkey, and then his mother served the pie.   (independent clause, independent clause)

Complex Sentence (Normal Order)

Walt ate the turkey before he ate the pie.   (main clause, dependent clause)

Miscellaneous Sentences

Walt ate the turkey, and his mother served the pie before he spoke. (independent clause, independent clause, dependent clause)

Walt hoped that his mother would serve pie.   (noun clause as direct object)

Walt loves eating turkey. (gerund phrase as direct object)

Walt thanked his mother for serving pie.   (gerund phrase as object of preposition)

Walt loves to eat turkey.   (infinitive phrase as direct object)

SENTENCE PATTERNS LESS COMMONLY USED BY STUDENTS

Simple Sentences (Inverted Order)

Slowly Walt ate.   (adverb, subject, verb)

The turkey Walt now ate.   (direct object, subject, adverb, verb)

Slowly Walt ate the turkey.   (adverb, subject, verb, direct object)

In a hurry Walt ate the turkey.   (prepositional phrase, subject, verb, direct object)

Basic to Thanksgiving dinner are turkey and pie.   (subjective complement, prepositional phrase, verb, subject, subject)

Complex Sentence (Inverted Order)

Before he ate the pie, Walt ate the turkey.   (dependent clause, main clause)
(Note that the comma is used only when the complex sentence is not in normal order.)

Miscellaneous Sentences

Having eaten the turkey, Walt started on the pie.   (introductory participial phrase)

Walt, having eaten the turkey, started on the pie.   (interrupting participial phrase)

Walt having eaten the turkey, his mother served the pie.   (introductory nominative absolute)

Walt, I believe, ate the turkey.   (simple sentence with parenthetical expression)

Walt, I believe, ate the turkey before he ate the pie.   (complex sentence with parenthetical expression)

That Walt ate the turkey is certain.   (noun clause as subject)

Walt gave the empty plate to his mother, who then washed it.   (adjective clause at end)

Walt, who ate the turkey, gave the empty plate to his mother.   (interrupting adjective clause)

Walt gave the empty plate to his mother, the cook.   (appositive at end)

Walt, a turkey lover, enjoyed his dinner.   (interrupting appositive)

Eating turkey is Walt's favorite pastime.   (gerund phrase as subject)

To eat turkey is Walt's favorite pastime.   (infinitive phrase as subject)

SENTENCE PATTERNS SELDOM USED BY STUDENTS

Balanced Sentences

Having eaten the turkey and having sniffed the aroma of pie from the kitchen, Walt settled back contentedly in his chair.   (two balanced introductory participial phrases)

Walt having eaten the turkey, and his mother having served the pie, dishwashing time approached.   (two balanced nominative absolutes)

That the dinner was one of the best he had ever eaten and that his mother was an outstanding cook were now certain to Walt.   (two balanced noun clauses as subjects)

Walt handed the dish to his mother, a cook who took pride in her work and who considered an empty plate the highest possible praise.   (appositive modified by two balanced adjective clauses)

Basic to anyone's Thanksgiving dinner but critical to Walt's are turkey and pie.   (two balanced subjective complements in inverted sentence)

More than anything Walt now wanted to settle back in his chair, to engage in polite conversation, and to forget the tower of dishes in the kitchen.   (three balanced infinitive phrases used as direct objects)

Walt hoped that there would be plenty of turkey left for a midnight snack and that his mother had put aside a piece of that delicious pie.   (two balanced noun clauses used as direct objects)

To get out of his chair or to approach the tower of dishes in the kitchen now seemed unthinkable to Walt, who settled back in his chair and waited for his mother to open the conversation. (two balanced infinitive phrases as subjects and an adjective clause containing two balanced verb phrases)

Balanced sentences present endless possibilities, of which but a few are listed here. For more about balance, see p. 156.

Emphasis

Contrary to what many students seem to think, the force of prose is weakened rather than strengthened by constant exclamation points, capital letters, underlined words, and intensifiers:

> Mindy looked perfectly *darling* in her red velvet! Red velvet is
> Big on the campus these days. Anyone who is Anyone has one!
> But red velvet was just *made* for Mindy. She is so gorgeous!

This degree of gushiness is most often confined, fortunately, to personal letters, sports columns, and society pages. But even so, beginning writers do not always employ the appropriate devices with which they might emphasize a word or idea. These are (1) pause, (2) position, and (3) repetition.

(1) *Emphasis by pause* makes use of the comma, dash, colon, semicolon, or period to set off an important idea:

> Each person is born to one possession which outvalues all his others—his last breath.
>
> Twain   *Pudd'nhead Wilson's
> New Calendar*

> By trying we can easily learn to endure adversity. Another man's, I mean.
>
> *Ibid.*

> In the first place God made idiots. This was for practice. Then he made School Boards.
>
> *Ibid.*

> There are people who can do all fine and heroic things but one: keep from telling their happinesses to the unhappy.
>
> *Ibid.*

(2) *Emphasis by position* may use an inverted sentence to call attention to a word or words which are displaced from their normal order.

Painfully he squirmed through the barbed wire.
Loud women I cannot stand.
Over the fence sailed the ball.

But the last word in a sentence is usually the most important because it will be remembered longest. Emphasis by position most often, therefore, will not change the sentence from its normal order but will merely save the most important idea until last. (This is called order of climax or climactic order.)

> I am a Jew. Hath not a Jew eyes? Hath not a Jew hands, organs, dimensions, affections, passions?
>
> > Shakespeare   *The Merchant of Venice*

> I know not what course others may take; but as for me, give me liberty, or give me death.
>
> > Patrick Henry, speech in the Virginia Convention, March, 1775

> Plato is dear to me, but dearer still is truth.
>
> > Aristotle

Aware of the importance of the end position, humorists will often make use of anti-climax by placing an unimportant idea after an important one.

(3) *Emphasis by repetition* requires special skill, for the tendency of too many writers is to leaden their prose with needless restatements of words and ideas. In the hands of an expert, however, repetition lends authority and majesty to composition:

> How do I love thee? Let me count the ways.
> I love thee to the depth and breadth and height
> My soul can reach, when feeling out of sight
> For the ends of Being and ideal Grace.
> I love thee to the level of every day's
> Most quiet need, by sun and candlelight.
> I love thee freely, as men strive for Right;
> I love thee purely, as they turn from Praise.
> I love thee with the passion put to use
> In my old griefs, and with my childhood's faith.

I love thee with a love I seemed to lose
With my lost saints,—I love thee with the breath,
Smiles, tears, of all my life!—and, if God choose,
I shall but love thee better after death.

> E. B. Browning *Sonnets from the*
> *Portuguese*

BALANCE

Of all the positive elements of style which you should strive for in your writing, the most important is balance. Sentence balance rests upon the grammatical principle of parallelism, which says that any items within a sentence which appear in a series or are joined by a coordinating conjunction must be expressed in the same form. Likewise, any items so expressed must contain ideas which are logically similar.

Constructions Lacking Parallelism	Improved Constructions
Dale invited Pat to go bowling and that they would have pizza afterward.	Dale invited Pat for bowling and pizza.
Kathy was hired to greet visitors, file clerk, and answering the telephone.	Kathy was hired to greet visitors, file, and answer the telephone.
Many students come to college for parties, athletics, and so they can join fraternities.	Many students come to college for parties, athletics and fraternity life.
Lorna is an attractive girl and who wears clothes well.	Lorna is an attractive girl who wears clothes well.

Ideas Lacking Parallelism	Improved Concepts
Common rodents are rats, squirrels, Mickey Mouse, beavers, and porcupines.	Common rodents are rats, squirrels, mice, beavers, and porcupines.
The youth was suntanned, tall, and good at surfing.	The suntanned, tall youth was good at surfing.

Dennis is a first string quarterback, serves as president of the student council, pops his gum noisily, but stars at track.

Dennis, who unfortunately pops his gum noisily, is a first string quarterback, serves as president of the student council, and stars at track.

The company vice president was loud, seemed uncertain of the social graces, had a mole below his left ear, and was rude to secretarial help.

The company vice president, who has a mole below his left ear, was loud, uncertain of the social graces, and rude to the secretaries.

But parallelism alone does not create the balanced rhythms which stir us in the great prose of writers like Faulkner, Steinbeck, Adlai Stevenson, and Winston Churchill. Balance is achieved through constructions which are not only parallel but which are fairly long and similar in movement:

The mature person is one who
accepts challenges with confidence,
lives in terms of tomorrow's satisfactions rather than
today's pleasures, and
loves other people because he has learned to love
himself.

Surely one of the great masterpieces of balanced prose is Lincoln's Gettysburg Address:

	Balanced Elements
Fourscore and	
seven	adjectives
years ago our fathers brought forth upon this	
continent a new nation,	
conceived in liberty, and	
dedicated to the proposition	participial phrases
that all men are created equal. Now we are	
engaged in a great civil war, testing whether	
that nation or	
any nation	nouns
so conceived and	
so dedicated	participles
can long endure.	

We are met on a great battlefield of that war. We have come to dedicate a portion of that field,	pronouns
as a final resting place for those who here gave their lives that that nation might live. It is altogether	
fitting and	
proper	adjectives
that we should do this. But, in a larger sense,	
we cannot dedicate—	
we cannot consecrate—	
we cannot hallow	independent clauses
this ground. The brave men	
living and	
dead	participles
who struggled here, have consecrated it, far above our poor power	
to add or	
detract.	infinitives
The world will little	
note nor long	
remember	verbs
what we say here,	
but it can never forget	
what they did here.	noun clauses
It is for us the living, rather	
to be dedicated here	
to the unfinished work	
which they who fought here have thus far so nobly advanced.	
It is rather for us	pronouns
to be here dedicated	infinitives
to the great task	prepositional phrases
remaining before us,—that	
from these honored dead	
we take increased devotion	
to that cause for which	prepositional phrases
they gave the last full measure	
of devotion—	clauses
that we here highly resolve	
that these dead shall not have died	
in vain—	

that this nation, under God, shall have
a new birth
of freedom—and   noun clauses
  that government
    of the people
    by the people
    for the people   prepositional phrases
shall not perish from the earth.

Once you are willing to examine the works of the best writers to study their techniques, you are on your way to developing those techniques for yourself. For no principle of writing discussed in this book is too difficult for the serious student who will put forth real effort.

Exercises

A. Sentence Clarity and Consistency

Rewrite the following sentences to improve any passages which are not clear or which contain shifts in person, voice, tense, or level of usage.

1. Becky met the mayor's wife who patted her head on Simpson Street.

2. Rinse the dishes with hot water, and then they can be more easily dried.

3. In Queen Victoria's day you wouldn't dream of wearing a bikini to the beach.

4. Janna lost her tooth in the apple with the gold filling.

5. I wonder if I should drop one of my classes this term because you don't learn anything when your schedule is too difficult.

6. After he returned the diamond necklace, the detective tells the heroine how he solves the crime.

7. The verdict of the psychiatrist is that his patient is nuts.

8. Frank described how he got the idea for his painting with many hand gestures.

9. After a lengthy deliberation the jury concluded Glenn bumped off the victim.

10. Whenever you visit Terri's house, your shoes must be taken off at the door.

B. Sentence Subordination (Participial Modifiers)

Combine the following pairs of sentences, putting the less important idea into a participial phrase.

1. Mike read the family history. It was written by his grandfather.

2. Dan was accepted by the newspaper. He will report for work Monday.

3. I was bored with my practicing. I decided to quit and go for a walk instead.

4. Robin likes steaks. They are broiled over hickory charcoal.

5. Myrna became irritated with the auctioneer. She refused to pay for the lamp.

6. We planted lawn seed two weeks ago. We are worried that it hasn't started to grow.

7. I have received an invitation to the Governor's Ball. I am trying to decide what to wear.

8. Jerry sneaked quietly into the kitchen. He hoped his mother wouldn't hear him.

9. Congressman Sloan walked down Main Street. He shook hands with people and urged them to vote for his re-election.

10. Kim was shocked by the newspaper account of the murder. She cancelled her subscription.

C. Sentence Subordination (All Dependent Constructions)

Combine the following groups of sentences, putting the main idea of each group in an independent clause and all other ideas in dependent constructions. Identify each dependent construction in the margin.

1. Wendy was frightened by the horror movie on television. She didn't sleep all night. She vowed never again to watch the Late Show.

2. I finished the book last night. I couldn't put it down. I was disappointed in the last chapter.

3. Lisa has a new coat. The coat is blue. She has more coats than anyone I know. This one isn't very flattering.

4. Last night I went to a party. It was a barbecue. It was very strange. The fish wasn't barbecued. It wasn't even cooked.

5. I can't decide what I want to be after I graduate. I have given up my desire to be an airline stewardess. I can't be a stewardess. I am not tall enough.

6. Mitchell is playing his new record. It is a rock and roll tune. The tune keeps repeating the same words and music. It is too loud. No one else in the family can stand rock and roll.

7. Arch builds furniture. This is his hobby. He made a coffee table. It looks like a cobbler's bench. He finished it last week.

8. Dorothy likes to bowl. She bowled last Wednesday. Her score was 127. Last year she averaged 110.

9. I have a headache. I bumped my head on the cupboard. Usually I get headaches when I don't eat.

10. Nancy was elected the new Homecoming Queen. She is very pretty. She was elected Homecoming Queen last year also. She is the only girl in the history of the school to be Homecoming Queen twice.

11. Chris is too fat. She lost eight pounds before Thanksgiving. She gained twelve pounds over the Christmas holidays.

12. I like all lilacs. My favorite lilacs are pink. I hope to plant many varieties of lilacs in my yard. I will probably use French hybrids.

13. Kim's parents think she talks too much. Her teacher sent a note home from school saying Kim was noisy in class. Kim is a good student. She likes school.

14. Joyce is not as pretty as her four sisters. People don't notice Joyce at first. Joyce writes good poetry. Joyce's soprano voice is thrilling to listen to.

15. Mr. Nolan teaches chemistry at Highland High School. He was my favorite teacher last year. He is getting married next week. He has invited me to the wedding.

D. Theme Assignment

Write a theme of 400-500 words on one of the following topics, paying attention to the elements of style discussed in Step 12.

I believe in God
I believe in pacifism
I believe in state's rights
I believe in federal support of schools
I believe in the U.N.
I believe in questioning authority
l believe in obedience
I believe in capital punishment
I believe in eliminating college grades
I believe in the spirit of Christmas
I believe in work
I believe in the importance of recreation
I believe in psychotherapy
I believe in exercise
I believe in keeping women in the homes
I believe in better work opportunities for women
I believe in restoring old landmarks
I believe in getting rid of slums

Postscript on Style and Tone

Step 12 examined certain qualities of writing identified as elements of style. These qualities are the ones which usually determine whether a given composition is effective or ineffective. But by no means are these the only qualities which will determine what overall impression your writing will make upon a reader. The ideas you set down will also reflect your own personality, and your prose may be—among other things—formal or informal, direct or indirect, logical or illogical, meaty or superficial, imaginative or factual.

Although you may not always be able to control every one of these qualities, you can decide whether you want a composition to be formal or informal. Most college themes and term papers should be somewhat formal. That means that they should follow most of the standards for formal writing listed below.

Formal Composition	Informal Composition
Uses exact and technical words	Uses short, common words
Uses long, balanced sentences	Uses short sentences or rambling sentences with many independent clauses joined by *and*'s and *but*'s
Alludes to history, literature, philosophy, mythology, the fine arts	Limits examples to material the layman can readily understand

Uses *he, one, they*	Uses *you, I, we*
Follows a clear method of organization	Strays from the most direct route
Employs conjunctive adverbs for transitions: *moreover, indeed, however, accordingly, nevertheless, therefore, consequently, hence, furthermore, otherwise*	Employs coordinating conjunctions for transitions: *but, and, yet, for, nor, or, so*
Maintains precise grammar including such technicalities as subjunctive verb mood	Imitates speech patterns
Spells out words	Uses contractions
Avoids colloquial expressions	Uses colloquialisms such as "flunk," "exam," "prof," "kind of" (meaning "rather"), "a lot" (meaning "many" or "much"), "complected," "enthused," "try and" (instead of "try to")

Formality or informality of writing cannot be judged by absolute standards since a composition may contain one or two words which alter the level slightly.

Another aspect of style which is highly personal is tone. Tone reflects the writer's attitudes—both toward his subject matter and toward his audience. For instance, the tone of an amused big brother would be quite different from the tone of a worried mother in advising a fifteen-year-old girl how to get along with boys. And both would adopt a still different tone with a five-year-old kindergarten girl whose boy friend had thrown a mud pie at her.

Tone, then, might convey your anger, amusement, reverence, gaiety, fear, irony, warmth, distress, or any other human emotion. But as much as the emotion itself, tone will reflect your tact in dealing with that emotion. The following quotations all express a general tone of satire. In other words, each holds up some human vice for ridicule. But in each one the satire is modified by varying degrees of bitterness, compassion, humor, despair, irritation, or cynicism.

If Heaven had looked upon riches to be a valuable thing, it
would not have given them to such a scoundrel.
        Swift   *Letter to Miss Vanhomrigh*

You have but a very few years to be young and handsome in the
eyes of the world; and as few months to be so in the eyes
of a husband, who is not a fool.
        Swift   *Letter to a Young Lady on her Marriage*

All kings is mostly rapscallions.
        Twain   *The Adventures of Huckleberry Finn*

They spell it Vinci and pronounce it Vinchy; foreigners always
spell better than they pronounce.
        Twain   *Innocents Abroad*

The louder he talked of his honour, the faster we counted our
spoons.
        Emerson   *Conduct of Life*

Beware when the great God lets loose a thinker on this planet.
        Emerson   *Essays*

Every hero becomes a bore at last.
        Emerson   *Essays*

It is said that God is always for the big battalions.
        Voltaire   *Lettres*

This world is a comedy to those that think, a tragedy to those
that feel.
        Walpole   *Letters*

A woman seldom asks advice before she has bought her wedding
clothes.
        Addison   *The Spectator*

Indeed I tremble for my country when I reflect that God is just.
        Jefferson   *Notes on Virginia*

Seldom are two passages ever identical in tone, but your general attitude must be consistent throughout a piece of writing. Furthermore, that attitude should be clearly established at the beginning of
a composition, preferably in the first sentence.

This discussion of tone holds the final position in this book not
because it occurred as an afterthought. On the contrary, tone was
reserved for this position because it is the one ingredient of writing

which you must always be aware of. A failure to do so can be disastrous, for an understanding of tone is critical not only to your own writing but to intelligent reading as well. Every piece of writing has some kind of tone, and the perceptive reader knows that the emotions with which words are set to paper are as important as the words themselves.

Checklist for Effectiveness

☐ 1. Have I eliminated the flapdoodle in my writing?
☐ 2. Have I made good use of sensory description?
☐ 3. Have I made sure that my figures of speech are not mixed, trite, unnatural, or habitual?
☐ 4. Am I guilty of substituting adjectives for nouns?
☐ 5. Are my adjectives and nouns concrete?
☐ 6. Are they fresh?
☐ 7. Have I crowded action into my sentences with adjectives formed from vigorous verbs?
☐ 8. Am I guilty of substituting adverbs for verbs?
☐ 9. Are my verbs specific?
☐ 10. Where possible, have I used action verbs instead of linking and passive ones?
☐ 11. Have I avoided repetition, jargon, general wordiness?
☐ 12. Is my writing clear?
☐ 13. Is it consistent?
☐ 14. Is it properly subordinated?
☐ 15. Is it varied?
☐ 16. Is it emphatic?
☐ 17. Is it balanced?
☐ 18. Have I established my tone in the first sentence and maintained it throughout my paper?

Index

abstract words, 83-84
action and active verbs
  exercise, 117-118
action and linking verbs, 107-109
active verbs, 108-109
Addison, Joseph
  quoted, 172
adjectives, 101-105
  vague, exercise, 113-114
adverbs, 105-106
alliteration, 135-136
allusion
  in formal composition, 170
amplified definition, 85
  exercise, 90-91
analogy, 78-80
analysis, 82-83
  exercises, 88-89, 90
  used in definition, 86-87
anecdote
  as conclusion, 31
anecdotes, 59-61
"and" or "but" before subordinating
  conjunctions, 149
apology
  a poor introduction, 29
arguing from analogy, 79
argumentative writing
  introduction for, 28

Aristotle
  quoted, 155
Arnold, Matthew
  quoted, 125
arrangement of ideas
  for coherence of whole paper, 32
  for coherence within paragraph, 50
arrangement of paragraph elements
  list of common methods, 59
assonance, 135
audience
  awareness of, 145, 150-151

balance, 153-154, 156-159, 170
beginnings (See *introductions*)
Bible, King James, 123, 144
  quoted, 106, 127
Boswell, James
  quoted, 106
Browning, Elizabeth Barrett
  quoted, 155-156
Browning, Robert
  quoted, 127, 136
Byron, George Gordon, Lord
  quoted, 124, 126, 127

"Calendar of Great Americans, A"
  exercise, 55-56

177

Canning, George
 quoted, 136
capitalization
 in formal outline, 20
Carroll, Lewis
 quoted, 106
cause to effect
 as reason, 93
 order, 67
checklist
 for effectiveness, 175
 for paragraphs, 97
 for patterns, 39
chronology, 60
Churchill, Winston, 157
clarity, 33, 144-145
 and consistency, exercise, 161-162
clauses
 coordinate, piling up of, 148-149
 dependent, piling up of, 148-150
climactic order, 66, 155
coherence, 32, 50
Coleridge, Samuel Taylor
 quoted, 124, 126, 127, 135, 137
colloquialisms
 in informal composition, 171
comparison and contrast, 77-79
 exercises, 80, 81
 used in definition, 86
complex material
 handled by analysis, 82
complex sentence, 151, 152
conclusion
 not always necessary, 30
 unmerited, 6
conclusions
 appropriate, 30-31
concrete writing, 102-103
conjunctions
 coordinating
  for transition, 51
  in informal composition, 171
 subordinating
  for transition, 51
 use of "and" and "but" before,
  149

conjunctive adverbs, 51
 in formal composition, 171
consistency, 145-148
 and clarity, exercise, 161-162
constructions, sentence
 variety in, 150-154
 weak, 144-150
contractions
 in informal composition, 171
controlling idea, 44-46, 72
 exercise, 54
coordinate clauses
 piling up of, 148-149
coordinating conjunctions
 in informal composition, 171
Cowper, William
 quoted, 123, 125, 126, 128, 129
crowding action into sentences, 104-
  105

definition, 83-88
 dictionary, 29
 exercises, 89, 90
dependent clauses
 piling up of, 148-150
description, 63-66
 exercise, 68-69
detail, 72-73, 75
 and illustration, exercises, 75, 76
diagram
 of poorly-organized theme, 6
 of verb effectiveness, 109
 of well-organized theme, 5
dictionary definition, 86-87
 a poor introduction, 29
dramatic incident
 as introduction, 28
division
 in formal outline, 20
Donne, John
 quoted, 126
Drayton, Michael
 quoted, 131

echo of the title
 a poor introduction, 29

effect to cause
  as reason, 94
effectiveness
  checklist for, 175
Emerson, Ralph Waldo
  quoted, 130, 131, 134, 172
emphasis, 154-156
  short paragraphs used for, 48
emphatic arrangement
  of ideas, exercise, 37
emphatic order
  within paragraphs, 59, 66
  within sentences, 155
empty writing, 71
examples
  must be related to generalizations,
    53
exclusion
  used in definition, 88
explicit thesis (see *thesis, placement
  of*)
exposition
  definition of, 3
  length of paragraphs for, 48-49
  primary aim of, 33
  sees with mind, 123
extended definition, 85
  exercise, 90-91

facts, 72-73, 75
  as opposed to reasons, 92, 94
Faulkner, William, 111, 122, 157
fiction
  length of paragraphs for, 47
figures of speech, 128-135
flabby verbs, 105-106
flair, 122
flapdoodle, 122
  definition of, 101
formal composition, 170-171
Franklin, Benjamin, 144

Gay, John
  quoted, 129
general and specific verbs, 107
  exercise, 115

generalizations, 70-72
  relating examples to, 53
"Gettysburg Address," 122, 144
  quoted, 31, 157-159
Gilbert, Sir William
  quoted, 134, 136
grammar
  precise in formal composition, 171
Gray, Thomas
  quoted, 124

habitual figures of speech, 135
Hale, Edward Everett, 144
he, one, they
  in formal composition, 171
Henry, Patrick
  quoted, 155
history
  used in definition, 87
hyperbole, 130

illustration, 72-75
  and detail, exercises, 75, 76
  used in definition, 85-86
images
  startling, 122
impressions
  sight, 123-124
  smell, 127-128
  sound, 124-125
  taste, 126-127
  touch, 125-126
informal composition, 170-171
introduction
  definition of, 25
introductions
  good, 26-28
    exercise, 35
  poor, 28-30
irony, 131-133

jargon, 110-111
Jefferson, Thomas
  quoted, 172

Keats, John
quoted, 123, 124, 125, 126, 127, 129
key terms
repetition of for translation, 51
key words (See *controlling idea*)
King James Bible, 123, 144
quoted, 106, 127
Kipling, Rudyard
quoted, 106, 129

level of usage
shifts in, 147-148
Lincoln, Abraham, 122, 144
quoted, 31, 157-159
linking and action verbs, 107-109
Locke, John, 111
logic
upside-down, 149
Lover, Samuel
quoted, 103
Lowell, James Russell
quoted, 131, 134

McGinley, Phyllis, 92
Macaulay, Thomas
quoted, 130
meaning
muddied by weak construction,
144-145
meaningless question
a poor introduction, 30
mechanical systems
for numbering paragraphs, 33
Melville, Herman, 122
metaphor, 128-129
Milton, John
quoted, 123, 125, 126, 131, 217
mixed figures of speech, 133-134
Much Ado About Nothing, The
a poor introduction, 29

narrative
within exposition, 18, 60-61
new material
never should be introduced in
conclusion, 31

newspaper stories
length of paragraphs for, 47
nouns, 101-104
vague, exercise, 113-114
obvious statements
should be discarded, 72
onomatopoeia, 136-137
order
of complexity, 67
of effectiveness of verbs, 108-109
paragraph, 59-67
organization
clear in formal composition, 171
methods of, 34
Otway, Thomas
quoted, 135
outline
formal, 19-21
informal, 13-18
exercise, 23
to be handed in, 21
Ovid
quoted, 102

paragraph
coherence within, 50
definition of, 49
exercise, 54
unity, 49-50
paragraphs
checklist for, 97
length of, 18, 46-49
parallelism, 156-157
for transition, 53
in formal topic outline, 21
participles, 104-105, 149-150
exercise, 163-164
passive verbs, 108-109, 146-147
pattern
formal outline as, 19-21
informal outline as, 13-18
thesis statement as, 3 ff.
topic sentence as, 43
patterns
checklist for, 39

patterns *(cont.)*
  sentence pattern commonly used by students, 151
  sentence pattern less commonly used by students, 152
  sentence pattern seldom used by students, 153
pause
  for emphasis, 154
person
  shifts in, 146
personification, 131
poetic devices, 122-137
  identification of, exercise, 139-141
"poetic" prose, 122-123
poetry
  techniques of, 122-123
Pope, Alexander
  quoted, 126
position
  for emphasis, 155
prejudices, 84-85
problem to solution
  as reason, 93
process, 59, 61-63
pronouns
  for transitions, 52-53
proof
  for topic sentences, 70-72
punctuation
  in formal outline, 20

question to answer
  as reason, 93
Quiller-Couch, Sir Arthur, 111
quotation
  as conclusion, 30
  as good introduction, 28

reasons, 92-94
  exercises, 94, 95
repetition
  for emphasis, 155-156
  of key terms
    for transition, 51
  thoughtless, 109-110

research paper
  outline for, 21
restatement of thesis
  as conclusion, 31
rhyme, 135
rhythm, 122-123, 157
Rossetti, Christina
  quoted, 129
"rubbish" verbs, 106
rules
  for avoiding wordiness and vagueness, 112
  for coherence, 32
  for formal outline, 19-21
  for informal outline, 14
  for paragraph coherence, 50-53
  for paragraph unity, 50
  for theme coherence, 34
  for thesis statement, 8-9
  for use of short paragraphs, 48-49

satire, 171-172
Scott, Sir Walter
  quoted, 136
sensory impressions, 123-127
  from vigorous adjectives, 104-105
sentence
  complex, 151, 152
  compound, 151, 152
  constructions
    variety in, 150-154
    weak, 144-150
  patterns
    commonly used by students, 151-152
    less commonly used by students, 152
    seldom used by students, 153
  that depends upon the title to be understood
    a poor introduction, 29
sentences
  balanced, 153-154
  in formal composition, 170
  short or rambling in informal composition, 170

sentences *(cont.)*
  simple, 151
    piling up of, 148-150
  upside-down, 148-150
Shakespeare, William
  quoted, 103, 106, 126, 127, 128,
    129, 130, 131, 134, 135, 136,
    137, 155
Shelley, Percy Bysshe
  quoted, 129
sight impressions, 123-124
simile, 129-130
simple sentences, 151
  piling up of, 148-150
smell impressions, 127
solution for problem presented in
  paper
  as conclusion, 31
sound impressions, 125-126
space order, 63-66
  exercise, 68-69
specific and general verbs, 107
statement designed to make reader
  think or act
  as conclusion, 31
statement designed to startle reader
  as introduction, 27
statement which anticipates reader's
  objections
  as introduction, 28
Steinbeck, John, 122, 157
Stevenson, Adlai, 157
style
  elements of, 101-112, 122-137, 144-
    159, 170-173
subject of paper
  selection of, 30
subjunctive verbs
  in formal composition, 171
subordinating conjunctions
  use of "and" or "but" before, 149
subordination, 148-150
  all dependent constructions, exer-
    cise, 165-168
  participial modifiers, exercise, 163-
    164

summary
  as conclusion for long paper, 31
  short paragraphs used for, 48
Surtees, Robert
  quoted, 132
Swift, Jonathan
  quoted, 133, 134, 172
synonyms
  for transition, 52

taste impressions, 126
Tennyson, Alfred, Lord
  quoted, 102, 125, 127, 129, 131, 136
tense
  shifts in, 147
thesis, 145
  accidental, 4-6
  compared to topic sentence, 43
  difference between thesis and the-
    sis statement, 14
  introduction to paper, 26-27
  placement of, 3, 9
thesis statement
  as pattern for theme, 3
  difference between topic and the-
    sis statement, 7
  examples of, 7, 13
  exercise, 11
  incorporated into introductory
    paragraph, 14
  qualities of, 7-8
Thomson, James
  quoted, 130
Tillich, Paul, 111
time order, 59-63
title
  echo of
    a poor introduction, 29
to be
  as a linking verb, 107-108
tone, 17, 171-173
  should be set in introduction, 25
topic
  difference between thesis state-
    ment and thesis, 7
  examples of, 7

topic *(cont.)*
  of current interest
    as good introduction, 28
topic sentence, 43-46
  as skeleton of paragraph, 70
  exercise, 54
topic sentences
  proof for, 70-72
touch impressions, 125-126
transition
  sentence
    may move topic sentence to second position, 46
    short paragraphs used for, 48
transitional connectives (See *conjunctive adverbs*)
transitional devices, 50-64
  recognizing, exercise, 55-56
  supplying, 57-58
transitional words and phrases, 50
transitions
  between paragraphs, 16, 17, 32-34
  inadequate, 53-54
trite adjectives, 104
trite figures of speech, 134
trivial statements
  should be discarded, 72
Twain, Mark, 101, 102
  quoted, 132, 154, 172
  quoted, exercise, 139-141

underlying idea (See *thesis*)
unfamiliar terms
  handled by analysis, 82-83
unity
  paragraph, 49-50
unnatural figures of speech, 134-135
upside-down sentences, 148-150
usage
  level of
    shifts in, 147-148

vague adjectives and nouns
  exercise, 113-114
vagueness, 101-112
  and wordiness, exercise, 119-120
variety, 150-154
Vaughan, Henry
  quoted, 129
verbs, 104-109
  action and active, exercise, 117-118
  adjectives derived from, 104-105, 149-150
  general, exercise, 115
  passive, 108-109, 146-147
  subjunctive in formal composition, 171
voice
  shifts in, 146-147
Voltaire
  quoted, 172

Waller, Edmund
  quoted, 128
Walpole, Horace
  quoted, 172
Whitman, Walt
  quoted, 124, 125, 126, 127, 128, 130, 131, 136, 137
Wilson, Woodrow
  quoted, exercise, 55-56
wordiness, 101-112
  and vagueness, exercise, 119-120
words
  abstract, 83-84
  in formal and informal composition, 170
  showy, 122
Wordsworth, William
  quoted, 124, 136

you, I, we
  in informal composition, 171